DEDICATION & ACKNOWLEDGEMENTS

For Gerry

I would especially like to thank:

– all who gave their time so generously to take part in the recordings.

– the always supportive and enthusiastic HarperCollins team: Nikki McMullan, Catherine Whitaker, Celia Wigley, Lorna McGavigan, and Lily Khambata.

– Teresa Miller from BMES, Bristol for her comments and probing questions during the writing process.

– my 'students' around the world (especially those from UPM) and from the Erasmus programme at the University of Bristol who have informed the writing of this book and who have given such valuable feedback on work in progress.

Thanks also to the following businesses for allowing us to make recordings of their employees:

Lawsons & Daughters, London
Cape Town Tourism, Cape Town
RSPB Vane Farm, Kinross
Vue Cinema
Tabard Inn, Washington, DC
Carhire 3000
Carphone Warehouse, Hammersmith
Thomas Exchange Global, London
Riverside Studios, London
Transport for London (Underground)
3AW radio station, Melbourne

About the author

Ian Badger is a highly regarded author who has written a wide range of published materials to aid spoken and written communication in English. He runs a training consultancy (BMES) which specialises in helping the employees of international companies to communicate with their counterparts, contacts, and customers worldwide. This work, which involves helping speakers from all over the world to communicate clearly and effectively with each other, has made him acutely aware of the need to understand English however it is spoken.

Ian is originally from London but now lives in Bristol in the west of England. He spends a lot of his time running face-to-face training in Finland, Germany, France, and Russia and working remotely in many other parts of the world. He has worked as a director of studies, teacher trainer, teacher of English, and communications consultant and is a regular speaker at international conferences.

Ian is also the author of *English for Business: Listening* (Collins, 2011).

Collins
English for Life

B1+ Intermediate

Listening

Ian Badger

Collins

HarperCollins Publishers
77-85 Fulham Palace Road
Hammersmith
London W6 8JB

First edition 2012

Reprint 10 9 8 7 6 5 4 3 2 1 0

Text © Ian Badger 2012
Audio recordings © HarperCollins Publishers
2012

ISBN 978-0-00-745872-1

Collins® is a registered trademark of
HarperCollins Publishers Limited.

www.collinselt.com

A catalogue record for this book is available
from the British Library.

Typeset in India by Aptara

Printed by South China Printing Co.

HarperCollins does not warrant that www.
collinselt.com or any other website mentioned
in this title will be provided uninterrupted, that
any website will be error free, that defects will
be corrected, or that the website or the server
that makes it available are free of viruses or
bugs. For full terms and conditions please refer
to the site terms provided on the website.

CONTENTS

INTRODUCTION

Collins English for Life: Listening will help you to improve your understanding of English as spoken by a range of speakers for whom it is a first or second language.

You can use *Listening*
- as a self-study course
- as supplementary material on a general English course.

Listening aims to develop your awareness and sensitivity to different speakers of English. As you listen to the recordings, you will note which speakers are easier to follow and notice why this is the case: speed, clear accent, lack of complex vocabulary and idiom, straightforward use of grammar. As you develop your awareness of features which make speakers easy to understand, you will gain more awareness of your own English and take steps to ensure that you become a clearer speaker.

Specifically, *Listening* will help you to develop:
- listening for the gist / the main points made by speakers
- listening for the exact meaning of words and phrases
- awareness of clear usage and structures
- your range of everyday English vocabulary
- cultural awareness

Listening comprises a **book** and **CD**. The **book** consists of 20 units, divided into the following five sections:

1 Where are you from?
2 Where are you going?
3 What do you need to know?
4 What do you do?
5 How do you spend your free time?

You can either work through the recordings from Unit 1 to Unit 20 or pick and choose the units that are most useful to you.

The **CD** contains 50 recordings of American, English, Irish, Scottish, Australian, New Zealand, French-Canadian, Chinese, German, and Polish speakers, among others. The ability to understand varieties of English is a key to improved communication in English in your work and leisure.

At the back of the book are the following useful documents:
- a mini-dictionary
- the answer key
- the transcripts for the audio recordings

Using *Listening*

For ease of use, each unit follows a similar structure. It is recommended that you follow the order of exercises when working through a unit. Each unit includes:
- Some simple questions to check your understanding of what is said.

- Exercises which focus on extracts from the recording where you can check your understanding of specific features: pronunciation, vocabulary, structure.
- Gap-filling exercises intended to direct your attention to specific words and phrases which may cause comprehension problems.
- Vocabulary-matching exercises to widen your vocabulary.

Some of the recordings will be difficult to understand at first, but the task will be to follow the main ideas expressed and to familiarize yourself with unfamiliar ways of speaking English. In cases where the language level of the exercises may appear low, understanding the gist and details of the recordings will present a challenge.

Other features

'Powered by COBUILD'

In order to extend your vocabulary, further uses of key language are explored through references to examples taken from the COBUILD corpus. In addition you can look up any unfamiliar words and phrases in the mini-dictionary at the back of the book. This contains definitions and further examples from a range of Collins COBUILD dictionaries.

Did you know?

Small sections set in speech bubbles provide useful background information which will help you to understand the context of a recording.

Clear usage

These sections focus on specific issues which can cause problems for the listener, such as complex grammar forms used by native speakers or non-standard usage.

Further listening

The final section in the each unit provides you with some suggestions for further study. In most cases it refers you to complimentary listening material on the *Collins Listening* website: www. collinselt.com/listening.

'We all make mistakes!'

'Since many years, I haven't seen a rifle in your hand!' From 'Fernando', ABBA

Native and very fluent non-native speakers make 'mistakes' – even ABBA. The recordings that accompany *Listening* were recorded on location (i.e. not in a studio) and are unscripted. As happens in the real world, the speakers make mistakes. They sometimes use unconventional grammar forms, they do not always speak in full sentences, and they hesitate. These 'errors' have not been removed from the recordings. The speakers' views are also unscripted and reflect their individual opinions and knowledge.

Language level

Listening has been written to help learners at B1–B2 level (intermediate), but will also be useful for learners at a higher level who wish to develop their sensitivity to a range of accents.

Other titles

Also available in the **Collins English for Life** series: **Speaking**, **Reading**, and **Writing**

Using the CD

This icon indicates that there is an audio track that you should listen to. Please note that the *Listening* CD is designed for use with a computer. If you want to play the audio on a CD player, you should download the tracks to your computer and then burn all of the tracks onto an audio CD.

1

YOUR FAMILY

The two speakers in this unit talk about their families. Before you listen, think about how you would talk about your family structure.

- Are you an only child or are you from a large family?
- Do you have many uncles and aunts, cousins, nieces and nephews?
- Are you close to your family or do you have little contact with family members?

A Alex is from a small English town in Derbyshire in the East Midlands. In this recording, he talks about his own family and his wife's family.

1 Read the questions and then play the recording through once. Answer the questions to check your general comprehension.

1 Do any of Alex's family members live within walking distance of where he lives?
2 How many of his wife's sisters (his sisters-in-law) have children?
3 Alex expresses regret that his and his wife's parents do not live nearby. Why?
4 How many brothers and sisters does Alex have?
5 Why is Alex happy to be part of his wife's larger family?

Useful vocabulary and phrases: family

Did you say you had ten siblings – seven brothers and three sisters?

All of my aunts and uncles came to the wedding. So did most of my cousins, my second cousins, my grandparents, and my great grandfather!

After remarrying, she now has four stepchildren: two stepsons and two stepdaughters.

My brother-in-law has two adopted children.

I have two half-sisters; we have the same mum but different dads.

Alex mentions a number of English places including Cornwall, a county in the far south west of England, and Derbyshire, a county in the Midlands. If you would like to explore the geography of the UK, locate the places mentioned on a map to give yourself a clearer idea of where the places are that Alex talks about. Go to **www.collinsmaps.com** and search for each one.

2 Now listen again, stop the recording as necessary, and complete the gaps in the sentences.

1 We don't really have any family in close ....
2 Mine are up in Derbyshire where I, where I ....
3 It is difficult not having any immediate family that you can rely on for ....
4 We make a conscious effort obviously to stay in touch with .... of our family.
5 I'm an .... I don't have any brothers or sisters.
6 To kind of become part of this big .... family [...] is really great.

Clear usage: talking about reoccurring events

Alex says:

'so we'll go up to Derbyshire'

Alex uses *will* in everyday speech to talk about what he does on a regular basis. *Will* can be used, particularly in spoken English, to express expected, habitual behaviour – it is not only used to refer to the future.

Note that Alex also says:

'My parents come down quite often.'

'We make a conscious effort to stay in touch.'

In these sentences, he uses the more widely used simple present to talk about regular behaviour and routines.

---

3 Listen to the recording one more time and identify words and phrases with similar meanings to the following words.

1 children   ....
2 all except   ....
3 very close family   ....
4 a serious effort   ....
5 looking after children   ....
6 depend on   ....

COBUILD CHECK: close

- Her grandmother and aunt live **close to** her.
- If your family doesn't live **close by**, weekends are the most practical time for visits.
- I have a number of **close relatives** and friends living in the area.
- We've always been a very **close family.**
- Over the next couple of months, we became **close friends.**
- I am **close to** my parents, my brother, and my sister.
- From the beginning he'd had a **close relationship** with his manager.

B In this recording, Patrick, who is from Southern Pines in North Carolina, USA, talks about the people who make up his extended family.

1 Read the questions and then play the recording. Are these statements true or false?

		True	False
1	Patrick has three siblings.		
2	His mother has several brothers and sisters.		
3	He has three uncles and three aunts.		
4	Elec is a common name in America.		
5	His grandmother remarried ten years after her divorce from his grandfather.		
6	His grandmother's new husband has not been welcomed into the family.		

> Patrick refers to his family as being like *The Brady Bunch*. This was an American TV series broadcast in the late 1960s / early 1970s about a large family that united when two widowed people remarried.
>
> Patrick also talks about his 'grandma' and 'grandpa'. Other informal words for grandparents include:
>
> 'gran' / 'granny' / 'nan'   'granddad' / 'gramps' / 'pop'

2 Now listen again and complete the following phrases.

1 My .... family isn't so big.

2 I have a brother and two step-sisters, as my mom is ....

3 We're anywhere from .... for a normal family gathering.

4 Obviously .... Alexander would be Alex.

5 My grandma is definitely .... of the family.

6 Don't get me wrong, she's a, she's a very loving ....

7 But every good divorce always leads to a better ....

8 She spent most of her life .... and has recently ....

COBUILD CHECK: family relationships

- 'How are you **related to** Hailey?'
- 'She is my **niece**, the **daughter** of my **sister**.'
- You and Robin are **second cousins**. Your fathers were **first cousins**.
- I got **married / remarried / divorced** twenty years ago.
- How long have you been **separated**?
- She **was widowed** five years ago.
- My uncle is a **widower**. His wife died last year.

3 Patrick uses a number of idiomatic phrases and sayings. Match the idiomatic expressions on the left with the simpler alternatives on the right.

1 as a matter of fact	please don't misunderstand me
2 isn't so big	well known for
3 loads and loads of	a well-respected man
4 don't get me wrong	a large number of
5 pretty famous for	actually
6 that's how we look at it	is not particularly big
7 a really good guy	that is our view

4 Find a word in the recording that means the same as the following.

1 strange   ....
2 get-together   ....
3 female ruler   ....
4 full stop   ....
5 challenge   ....
6 enormous   ....

Clear usage: 'imagine' and 'suppose'

Note how Patrick uses these two verbs to qualify his statements. By using such language, he softens the impact of what he says and helps to involve and include the listener.

'I imagine we're anywhere from twenty to fifty for a normal family gathering.'

'So if you can imagine that ...'

'I suppose that's how we look at it.'

'Just after my mom turned eighteen, I would imagine.'

Some other examples:

I suppose you could say that we are a close family.

I suppose we should leave now.

I imagine that some people would see us as unusual.

I can't imagine that the party will finish early.

FURTHER LISTENING

Listen to the recordings again and read through the transcripts. For further recordings of Alex and Patrick, go to the website **www.collinselt.com/listening**.

2 YOUR HOME TOWN

BEFORE YOU LISTEN

In this unit, the two speakers describe their very different 'home towns'.

- How would you describe your home town (or village, city, or area where you live)?
- If asked to introduce the place where you live, would you focus on the landscape, the people, the atmosphere?

A Tonya lives in Georgia in the American South. In this recording, she talks about her home town – the city of Atlanta.

1 Read through the statements below and then play the recording through once. Are the statements true or false?

	True	False
1 Atlanta is no longer a 'green' city as many trees have been cut down.		
2 A large proportion of Atlanta's population has moved to Atlanta – they were not born there.		
3 The rail system is very well used in Atlanta.		
4 Tonya drives to work every day.		

A 'surface street' in US English is a standard local road. The term is used to differentiate this type of road from 'a freeway' and not, as you might guess, as a comparison with travelling underground.

Tonya talks about the 'railroad' in Atlanta. Note these US / UK differences in transport vocabulary:

US	UK	US	UK
railroad	railway	freeway / highway	motorway
track (in the station)	platform	gas / gasoline	petrol
sidewalk	pavement	(traffic) circle	roundabout
pavement	tarmac	intersection	junction
parking lot	car park	divided highway	dual carriageway

2 **Now listen again, pause the recording as necessary and fill in the gaps in these sentences.**

1   Atlanta, Georgia is a .... city.

2   In Atlanta I think we've done a .... of maintaining the greenery in our city.

3   It is a .... city.

4   We're a city of transplants, which makes us .... diverse.

5   I know a few people who .... into work.

6   So we've .... do something about transportation.

Tonya says:

'Something that we're really good at in the States is, when a city is being developed, taking all the trees out – just bulldozing them.'

Although she says they're 'really good at' it, is Tonya proud of this? Or is she being ironic?

Also note her use of *great* – 'a great job', and 'a really great city'. How do you respond to hearing such language?

Note that in some cultures, overusing (or underusing) such enthusiastic language can have a negative impact on conversation. Think about what level is appropriate where you live. Do you use enough enthusiastic language? Do you use too much?

3 **Match the words taken from the recording (on the left) with the word or phrase that has a similar meaning (on the right).**

1   develop   a   can't manage without

2   maintain   b   varied

3   rely on   c   expand

4   diverse   d   keep

5   drive to and from   e   use

6   utilize   f   commute

Clear usage: present passive continuous

Note how Tonya uses the passive continuous form of the present tense to describe *what is being done currently*:

'When a city is being developed' = When they are developing the city (*active form*)

Some other examples:

Trees are being cut down.

Houses are being bulldozed.

A transport system is being utilized.

Shops are being closed.

B Alex, who also featured in unit 1, lives in the countryside near London. In this recording, he talks about where he lives.

1 Read the general comprehension questions below. Then play the recording through once and answer the questions.

1 What kind of place does Alex live in?

2 Which part of England does Alex say he lives in?

3 Where would Alex ideally like to live?

4 How long does it take him to drive into London?

Alex mentions 'the Lake District'. The Lake District is a national park in the north west of England to the north of the city of Manchester. The Lake District covers an area of 2,292 square kilometres or 885 square miles and is known for its beautiful mountains and lakes. Tourists visit the Lake District in large numbers to enjoy activities such as hiking, bird watching and fishing. Many people also visit the area simply to enjoy the beautiful scenery.

---

2 Now listen again and complete the phrases.

1 I live with my family – wife and two kids in a ....

2 So you wouldn't really call it, kind of, ...

3 There is a large amount of common land and .... that you can go in.

4 You would never feel that you were in the ...., as you might do if you were in Scotland.

5 We've never, I suppose, had the .... or the jobs to allow us to, kind of, make that break.

6 The great thing about .... is we can ...

7 I drive into the— sort of West London which ...., you know, about an hour.

8 Or you can drive .... and be in the centre of London in half an hour.

Clear usage: talking about the past and the future

Notice the language Alex uses to focus on where *he has lived*:

'That's always where *I've lived*.'

'*I've always lived* around that area.'

'*We've never had* the courage to make that break.'

and where he *would like to live*:

'*We'd probably quite like to live* in the middle of nowhere.'

Where have you lived and where would you like to live?

3 Which of these statements best describes Alex's attitude to where he lives near London? Can you explain why he feels the way he does?

1 He hates it.

2 He loves it.

3 It is not convenient for his work in London.

4 It is not where he would live if he had free choice.

Alex says that he lives in a 'largish village'. 'Largish' means 'quite large'. Note that '-ish' is sometime added to some other adjectives in everyday informal English to replace 'quite' or 'fairly' – but be careful about using it because many speakers of English do not really like it! They find it too casual and informal.

It is a smallish community.

She has beautiful, long, reddish hair.

They said the exam was easyish but let's see how the results look.

4 Match the word taken from the recording (on the left) with the word or phrase that has a similar meaning (on the right).

1	village	a	bravery
2	middle of nowhere	b	choice
3	decision	c	very small town
4	rural	d	countryside
5	location	e	very remote place
6	courage	f	place

COBUILD CHECK: town and country

- He grew up in Chicago's western **suburbs**.
- The street where she lived was on the **outskirts** of the city.
- Most will probably wish to get out of this busy **urban** sprawl into the hills or to smaller coastal villages.
- The speed limit in **built-up** areas is 60 km per hour.
- The buildings in the **inner city** tend to be high density.

FURTHER LISTENING

Listen to the recordings again and read through the transcripts. For further recordings of Tonya and Alex and other speakers talking about their home towns, go to the website, **www.collinselt.com/listening**.

3 YOUR COUNTRY

BEFORE YOU LISTEN

The two speakers in this unit talk about their home countries.

- What features of your country are particularly unique?
- How would you compare the country where you live with other countries where you have lived or which you have visited?

A **Liz is from Tauranga, a small town on the North Island of New Zealand. In this recording she talks about the differences she sees between Australia and New Zealand.**

1 **Play the recording through once. Are these statements true or false?**

	True	False
1 Liz used to think that the landscape in Australia and New Zealand was similar.		
2 Both countries are inhabited by fierce and frightening animals.		
3 Most of the inhabitants of New Zealand originally came from the UK.		
4 The Maoris, the indigenous people of New Zealand, are thought to have arrived in the country by boat from Hawaii.		

Liz describes some New Zealand and Australian animal life and landscapes. Refer to the mini-dictionary (page 84) to check that you understand the following terms: 'lush', 'eucalyptus trees', and 'terrain'.

2 **Now read aloud the following words and phrases. Underline any words or phrases which you find difficult to understand. Then play the recording again and familiarize yourself with the way Liz pronounces these in a New Zealand accent. Note, for example, how she pronounces the word 'head' (usually pronounced _hed_) more like _hid_.**

Australia's quite red and the trees aren't very bushy.

New Zealand's got bushy trees with lots of birds and insects, but no scary animals.

Australia looks more barren, but it's really beautiful as well.

New Zealand is basically all made up of immigrants from the UK.

When I was growing up, it was a lot more just Europeans from the UK.

I don't think [they] had encountered anybody for a long time until Europeans went there.

It is still a two and a half hour flight from New Zealand to Australia.

COBUILD CHECK: people

- The Maori are **indigenous people** of New Zealand who founded a rugby team in 1910 to stop their players from heading to an Australian league.
- Without new **immigrants**, the work force in Toronto and Montreal would have shrunk.
- These Cuban-Americans consider themselves traditional economic **migrants**, as opposed to political **refugees**.
- Some of the **asylum seekers** will have experienced torture in their home country.
- Other **refugees** are being accommodated in Italy, France, and Greece and some **are settling** in countries in eastern Europe.

3 **Now listen again, stop the recording as necessary and complete the gaps in the sentences.**

1 When I went to Australia .... 'cos I too was expecting it to be quite similar.

2 New Zealand just has the birds and ....

3 Australia's got a large ….................... community and …................... community.

4 They were more ….................... at warfare than the indigenous people in Australia.

5 They communicated a lot differently and they ….................... and ...

6 ... from New Zealand to Australia. They're not ….................... .

Clear usage: modifying language

Note the way Liz frequently uses modifying language as she speaks: *quite; really; very; very, very;* (and even *long, long*!) for emphasis:

'Australia and New Zealand are *quite* different, even terrain-wise.'

'I too was expecting it to be *quite* similar.'

'Australia looks more barren, but it's *really* beautiful.'

'There [are] *quite* a lot of Asians [...] that have come from Japan and Malaysia.'

'The indigenous people in Australia have been there for a *very, very* long time.'

'[They] have lived in the desert for a *long, long* time.'

4 **Match the verbs vocabulary taken from the recording (on the left) with words that have similar meanings (on the right).**

1	indigenous	a	fierce
2	immigrant	b	people who have moved
3	terrain	c	frightening
4	ferocious	d	native
5	encounter	e	landscape
6	scary	f	meet

B Stella is originally from Hong Kong and now lives in Beijing. In this recording, she talks about everyday life in China and makes recommendations for visitors to the country.

1 Listen to the recording. Which of the statements below are true and which are false?

	True	False
1 Stella thinks you can learn a lot about China before you come to the country.		
2 Nearly all luxury goods are available in China.		
3 Prices in China are often very low.		
4 Stella strongly recommends that visitors to China visit the Forbidden City and the Great Wall so that they can buy interesting souvenirs.		
5 According to Stella, karaoke is popular with everyone in China, not just with young people.		

Certain aspects of Stella's English are not 'standard'. Do these features cause you difficulty in understanding her? Do other features of her speech cause you problems?

1 'The thing it's' = *The thing is ...*

2 'When people came' = *When people come*

3 'In the past, you can hardly see' = *In the past, you could hardly see*

4 'We'll took them' = *We'll take them*

5 'cheap', usually pronounced with a long *ee* sound, is pronounced *chip* by Stella

Stella talks about how important it is for visitors to China to visit the most important and famous historical sites, such as the Forbidden City and the Great Wall, in order to understand Chinese history and consequently the Chinese 'mindset'. She believes that you can only understand modern China by having an understanding of its history.

The Forbidden City in central Beijing was built between 1406 and 1420 and is a complex which consists of 980 buildings. For many years, it was the home of Chinese emperors.

The Great Wall of China was originally constructed to protect the northern borders of the Chinese Empire and was built and rebuilt between the fifth century BC and the sixteenth century.

2 Now listen again and focus on the phrases below. As you listen, underline any words that you find difficult to understand, and then familiarize yourself with Stella's pronunciation.

It's a very big difference in cultures with the Western world.

I think there are things that you can show to them. It's, you know, like shopping.

In the past, you can [could] hardly see any luxurious good(s).

But now it's— all the brands are there.

It's a city of variety and diversity as well, you know.

Then you can understand the Chinese history.

This is what modern China [Chinese] people, you know, enjoy.

3 **Now listen once more. Pause the recording as necessary and fill in the gaps.**

1   You cannot learn about China from a ....

2   'Cos they can see the .... in shopping.

3   It's a city of variety and .... as well, you know.

4   You need to .... Then you can understand the Chinese history.

5   .... is the place that they can say, 'Okay, this is what modern [Chinese] people enjoy'.

6   It's not only for .... people, it's for everyone.

COBUILD CHECK: culture

- The children come from **a variety of** religious backgrounds.
- To be Australian is to respect **a diversity of** cultures, because we are a mix of cultures.
- This will help them understand the unique Aboriginal **mindset**, culture, and world-view.
- Our cultural **heritage** goes back more than a thousand years.
- When different **cultures** come into contact with one another, the potential for confusion and conflict multiplies.
- The Forbidden City in Beijing is a World Heritage site at the very heart of Chinese **culture** and **history**.

After you listen

- Does anything surprise you about what Stella says about Beijing?
- What questions would you like to ask her?
- How easy is it for you to understand Stella? Have you met any Chinese people before? How does her English compare with other Chinese speakers you have met?

FURTHER LISTENING

Listen to the recordings again and read through the transcripts. For further recordings go to the website: **www.collinselt.com/listening**.

4 HOUSING AND ACCOMMODATION

BEFORE YOU LISTEN

In this unit, you will hear two very different recordings concerning housing (and household help).

- How you would describe where you live to someone who was coming to stay with you?
- What do you like most about your house / flat?
- What features of your house / flat do other people like most?
- Do you do your own housework? Do you have outside help?
- Think about the household chores that need to be done – cleaning, washing, cooking, gardening. How would you talk about the jobs that need to be done in your home on a day-to-day basis?

A In the first recording in this unit, an estate agent describes some properties to someone interested in renting.

1 Listen to the recording and complete the information in the table below based on the information given. Note that the agent says he has two properties at the beginning of the recording, but he actually describes three.

Information	Property 1	Property 2	Property 3
Number of bedrooms			
Number of floors			
Number of bathrooms			
Garden?	Yes / No / Don't know	Yes / No / Don't know	Yes / No / Don't know
Balcony?	Yes / No / Don't know	Yes / No / Don't know	Yes / No / Don't know
Views?	Yes / No / Don't know	Yes / No / Don't know	Yes / No / Don't know
Car parking?	Yes / No / Don't know	Yes / No / Don't know	Yes / No / Don't know
Gated?	Yes / No / Don't know	Yes / No / Don't know	Yes / No / Don't know

2 Now listen again. Complete the phrases to check your detailed listening.

Property 1

1 I've got one that's a .... house.

2 It's recently refurbished, so it's got a .... kitchen.

3 The rear garden is .... so obviously you'll get the sun most of the day.

4 It's still large enough to fit a .... and a wardrobe.

Property 2

1 It's not a house, but it's actually a riverside ....

2 It's a gated development with .... porterage.

3 There's a .... that overlooks the river.

4 It's got an .... space with it.

Useful vocabulary and phrases: asking about houses and furniture

How many *bedrooms* did you say there were in the house? (living rooms / kitchens / bathrooms / cloakrooms / staircases)

Is there a *separate bathroom*? (separate toilet / en-suite bathroom / store room)

Is there much *wardrobe* space? (cupboard / shelf / wall)

Are the *sofas* staying in the flat or will I need to buy new ones?
(armchairs / cupboards / shelves / curtains / blinds)

Always check which floor you are talking about to avoid confusion!
The UK ground floor = the first floor in many other countries.

COBUILD CHECK: housing

- It was a fine **terraced house** with three stone steps up to the front door.
- Roughly one in three of all new **detached houses** and **bungalows** are built by the people who are going to live in them.
- A two-bedroom, first- and second-floor **maisonette** in a Georgian **town house** is now available to let for £1,200 per month.
- There is no great difference in rental prices between **furnished** and **unfurnished** houses or apartments.
- We bought a recently **refurbished** house in Holland Park, Kensington.

3 Play the recording again and this time listen out for the renter's questions and comments as she listens actively to the estate agent. Complete the phrases below:

1 .... there was another property?

2 Right, ... Just out of interest, are there any flats in the area?

3 And .... the bedrooms in that one?

4 For ...., were they furnished or unfurnished, part-furnished?

After you listen

- Which of the properties described by the estate agent appealed to you most?
- Do you have other requirements?
- If you do not know other English words for rooms, furniture, or location in English, check them in your dictionary.

B In this recording, Gayatri, who is originally from India but now lives in the UK, talks about the importance of household help in India.

1 Read these general comprehension questions first. Then play the recording through once and answer each question.

1 Does Gayatri think that having household help in India is only a luxury?
2 What does she say would happen to you if you had to clean and scrub all day?
3 How are things changing in Indian cities with regard to household help?
4 In India, what kinds of jobs does the family's local handyman do?

Gayatri says:

'You *would die* if you had to clean and scrub every day.'

This sounds a little exaggerated even if the use of the conditional form of the verb is correct. Some more down-to-earth examples:

If you had to work for twelve hours a day in those conditions, you would be very tired.
If I had to do that work, I wouldn't be happy.

2 Now listen again. Complete the phrases for detailed listening practice.

1 You have …..................… help. You have somebody to cook for you.
2 It's also a means of …... to somebody.
3 The houses in India are …..................… for self-maintenance.
4 In India you need …..................… maybe twice a day.
5 The more help you have, …..................… people you have to manage.

Clear usage: word stress and repetition

Notice how Gayatri stresses certain words and phrases to underline her most important points. Note also the way she repeats phrases to make her key points stronger:

'*You have* household help. *You have* somebody to cook for you.'
'*It's not just* about— In India, *it's not just* about having the help. *It's not* a luxury.'
'*You need* to dust every day. Here *you don't really need* to dust everyday, but in India *you need* to dust maybe twice a day.'

Useful vocabulary and phrases: household appliances and household chores

refrigerator (fridge)	cleaning
freezer	scrubbing
vacuum cleaner	dusting
dishwasher	wiping
washing machine	washing up
kitchen sink	vacuuming
boiler	cooking
heater	mending
radiator	tidying up
cooker	mopping

---

3 Match the person (on the left) with the task that they might help with (on the right). Of course, most of us do not have the luxury of asking for help but would do many of these jobs ourselves!

1	a plumber	**a**	a broken satellite box
2	a cleaner	**b**	a gate that needs fixing
3	an electrician	**c**	a dirty oven
4	a TV repairman	**d**	a lawn that needs mowing
5	a handyman	**e**	problems with some wiring
6	a gardener	**f**	a leaking tap

COBUILD CHECK: help in the home

- We recently hired a **handyman** to do some work around our house.
- Mains lighting should be installed by a qualified **electrician**.
- She called a **plumber** to fix the washing machine at her new flat.
- I've arranged for a firm of landscape **gardeners** to come in later today.
- **Nannies** and **cleaners** are the fastest-growing sector of our economy: working mothers spend 90 per cent of their salaries on keeping the household running.
- She had hoped he would help with some **household chores**.

FURTHER LISTENING

Listen to the recordings again and read through the transcripts. For further housing-related recordings and for more of Gayatri, go to **www.collinselt.com/listening**.

5 ADAPTING TO LOCAL CUSTOMS

The speakers in this unit describe their experience of living in other countries.

- Have you ever moved from one country to another?
- Have you ever moved from one region / town in your own country to another?
- How would you describe your experience of having to adapt?
- What would you do to make sure you got the most from an experience of spending time living in another country?

A Gayatri is originally from Kashmir in India but has lived in the UK for many years. In this recording, she talks about her experience of being an Indian in the UK.

1 Read the statements below. Then, play the recording through once. Are the statements true or false?

	True	False
1 Gayatri enjoys her life as a Sikh living in London.		
2 The Sikh New Year is celebrated in London.		
3 Gayatri celebrates this festival surrounded by all of her family.		
4 She and her family are sometimes confused about which language to speak together.		
5 She is delighted when her daughter answers her in a 'totally British' accent.		

Gayatri, a member of the Sikh faith, mentions the *Vaisakhi* festival. This festival is a very significant event in the Sikh calendar. It is an ancient festival to celebrate the Sikh New Year and to commemorate the establishment of the Sikh religion. It is also celebrated (to a lesser extent) by non-Sikhs in India as a harvest festival. It normally takes place on 13th or 14th April.

Gayatri also mentions Ken Livingstone, a former mayor of London.

2 Now listen again, stop the recording as necessary, and complete the gaps in the sentences.

1 Because in some ways we get the .... worlds.

2   We try and go there regularly [...] on weekends .... in the community gathering.

3   One of our Sikh New Years is actually .... in Trafalgar Square every year.

4   What I .... is not having family around to enjoy it with.

5   It can be a .... because we are trying to teach our children our language.

6   So they're growing up a little bit .... as well.

 3   **Match the verbs taken from the recording (on the left) with words that have similar meanings (on the right).**

1 mix up		**a**	fit in
2 struggle		**b**	confuse
3 celebrate		**c**	make compulsory
4 enforce		**d**	enjoy oneself
5 take offence		**e**	have difficulty
6 integrate		**f**	feel someone has done you wrong

COBUILD CHECK: fitting in

- You have to **fit in** with this **culture** in order to get on. And that means you've got to compromise a bit.
- I went over there with the attitude that I'd learn the language and try to **adapt** to the **way of life**.
- All immigrants coming to the United States face the challenge of **adjusting** their native culture and **customs** to the **mores** of the new land.
- No one spoke English and I really **made an effort** to **integrate** with the locals.
- Tourists going to foreign countries should **familiarize themselves with** the cultures they will be visiting.
- The area is ethnically **mixed**, including a substantial North African community.
- The chalet holds about 19 people, and in any one week there'll be **a mixed bag** of couples, groups and singles.
- Since then, the number of **asylum seekers** has increased.

B   **In this recording, Lisa, who studied Spanish at university, talks about how she tried to integrate into Spanish life when spending a year abroad there as part of her studies.**

1   **Read the general comprehension questions below. Then play the recording through once and answer the questions.**

1   Who did Lisa live with when she was in Spain?

2   What was the most difficult thing she had to face when moving to Spain – finding somewhere to live or understanding the housing contract?

3   What was her landlady's attitude towards Lisa's difficulties in understanding the contract?

4   What are the main objectives of having a year abroad, in Lisa's opinion?

2 Now listen again. Complete the phrases and check the meaning of any language you do not know in the mini-dictionary.

1 I didn't just stay with them and form a clique and not .... the Spanish people.
2 I lived with two Spanish girls which was .... at first.
3 In the beginning they .... speak really slowly and [loudly].
4 She didn't really understand why I couldn't understand what I ....
5 You have to .... when you're over there.
6 Just talk to locals and learn (as much) as many .... phrases.

Lisa uses some informal spoken language, known as 'colloquial language'. She also says she was keen to learn the colloquial language of Spain when she lived there too. Many colloquial expressions cannot be found in standard dictionaries. When you are living in a particular country, it is valuable to learn the local colloquial language. However, you need to take care about using such language when you are using the language in an international context and you want to be clearly understood.

Here are some examples of Lisa's 'colloquial language' with some suggestions for more formal alternatives in brackets:

'I often felt like a bit of an idiot.' = *I often felt rather stupid.*

'I didn't understand the contract at all, 'cos it was all legal terms.' = *I didn't understand the contract at all, because everything was written in legal terminology.*

3 In which order do the following phrases appear in the recording? Check that you understand what each one means. Can the context help you?

1 the objective of your year abroad
2 those are the kinds of challenges you face
3 sometimes I might not know what to say in response
4 we got on really well
5 so that I didn't just speak English all the time
6 the most difficult thing when I first arrived   ....

COBUILD CHECK: feeling welcome

- The people there were extremely **welcoming** and extremely generous.
- We weren't expecting such a **warm reception**.
- We had a **hostile reception** from customs officers, who were **rude** and **offensive**.
- A warm, **hospitable** welcome is the hallmark of island people in general.
- You have to settle and **embrace the culture**.
- We should **celebrate** the traditional culture here.
- It was quite a **daunting** experience, but also a fascinating challenge.

C Kara and Jeremy, originally from New York and Los Angeles respectively, both currently work in the UK. In this recording, they discuss how social norms surrounding such essentials as tea- and coffee-drinking differ in the UK compared with their experience in the USA.

1 Play the recording through once. Are the following statements true or false?

		True	False
1	Jeremy wants to get involved in what he describes as the 'tea cycle' in his UK office.		
2	It is normal practice to make a pot of coffee just for yourself in an office in the USA.		
3	People drink tea in American offices.		
4	People get upset if you do not offer to make them coffee in an American office.		

Jeremy says:

'It's just too much pressure for me, to get involved in this tea cycle.'

Jeremy is speaking 'tongue in cheek' – he is pretending to be annoyed, but he is not being serious.

Note also that he uses the present continuous tense 'you are getting asked' which is often used to express a degree of irritation. This form is far more emphatic than the simple present *you get asked* or *you are asked*.

2 Now listen again, stop the recording as necessary, and complete the gaps in the sentences. Note the verb forms used:

1 And then it .... throughout the day.
2 You could drink up to five, maybe eight cups of tea in a day if you were ....
3 So what do you do when you're back in the States, you .... tea?
4 Yeah, you .... it for other people.
5 Everyone else gets their own. .... to your own devices.

After you listen

Reflect on the language Jeremy and Kara use to discuss their experience of UK tea culture. Compare the actual language they use with the friendly sentiments behind their words.

FURTHER LISTENING

Listen to the recordings again and read through the transcripts. For further recordings of all of the speakers in this unit, go to the website **www.collinselt.com/listening**.

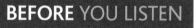

6 TOURIST INFORMATION

BEFORE YOU LISTEN

This unit features two very different recordings of enquiry phone calls. One is to the Cape Town tourist office in South Africa and the other is to a bird-watching reserve in Scotland.

- Where do you like to go on holiday?
- How do you find out about the places you want to visit?
- Do you enjoy being a tourist in a foreign country or do you find it daunting? Why?

A In this recording, Jessica, who works for Cape Town Tourism, recommends the main tourist attractions in Cape Town, South Africa, to Celia, who would like to have a holiday there.

1 Play the recording through once. Are these statements true or false?

	True	False
1 The Table Mountain aerial cableway is one of the 'top six' attractions.		
2 The Castle of Good Hope is not in the 'top six' attractions and is not worth seeing.		
3 If you want to visit Robben Island, you just turn up and go.		
4 A tour of Robben Island takes three hours and thirty minutes.		

2 Now listen again, listening in particular for the following words and phrases. Underline any words you do not understand. Familiarize yourself with Jessica's South African accent and the way she pronounces her 'e' and 'a' sounds in words such as *attractions, example, recommend, depend.*

Then you also have, for example, your Kirstenbosch Botanical Gardens.

Those would be the top attractions in Cape Town.

The other ones that I can also add ...

Some of the must-see attractions that I would recommend you to see ...

It does also depend on what your preferences are.

It's a very, very popular tourist attraction ...

You take a ferry ride to the island and back.

Robben Island – the island off the coast of Cape Town where Nelson Mandela was imprisoned.

The Constantia winelands – an area of vineyards close to Cape Town.

If you are interested in learning about South Africa, go online to check details of the places in Cape Town mentioned by Jessica. You can also locate some of them on the map by going to **www.collinsmaps.com** and searching for 'Cape Town'.

COBUILD CHECK: being a tourist

- The museum has become one of the city's most popular **tourist attractions**.
- You might have to **book in advance** and will probably have to pay an admission fee.
- At the end of the trip, we have a day free for some last minute **sightseeing** and shopping.
- The island of Capri is a twenty-minute **ferry ride** from Sorrento.

3 Now listen again, stop the recording as necessary and this time complete the phrases that Celia uses to demonstrate her active listening and to encourage Jessica to say more:

1 **Jessica:** The 'big six' which are the top six attractions …
  Celia: ....

2 **Jessica:** As well as also Robben Island. Okay, so …
  Celia: ....

3 **Jessica:** … that I would recommend you to see when you do come to Cape Town.
  Celia: ....

4 **Jessica:** You know, outdoor activities …
  Celia: .... a mix from my point of view.

5 **Jessica:** It's a very, very popular tourist attraction …
  Celia: ....

Clear usage: 'recommend'

Note how Jessica recommends her favourite attractions to Celia:

'It's *definitely recommended*'

'The must-see attractions that *I would recommend you to see*' (non-standard English, but in common use)

Other uses of *recommend*:

I recommend that you take a trip to the winelands.

I recommend taking the cable car to the top of Table Mountain.

What would you recommend?

Do you have any recommendations?

B In this telephone recording, Lorna phones Vane Farm, a venue for bird-watching near her home town in Scotland, to ask for details of opening times and facilities. Leon answers the phone. Note that there is some noise in Leon's office which can be heard in the background.

1 Read the general comprehension questions below. Then play the recording through once and answer each question.

1 When does the café open and close?
2 How much will it cost Lorna's grandmother to get in?
3 Which member of the group mentioned is a member of the RSPB?
4 Will it be difficult for a wheelchair-user to access the café?
5 Why will it be difficult for her grandmother to explore the whole reserve?

The 'RSPB' (the Royal Society for the Protection of Birds) is a UK-based charity.

Lorna is looking forward to having 'a cup of tea and a scone' at Vane Farm. A 'scone' is a special kind of cake usually eaten with butter which is a tea-time treat in the UK.

'OAP' (old age pensioner) is a term used for people in the UK who are over the age of 65 and who are retired. Another slightly more polite term is *senior citizen*.

Useful vocabulary and phrases: checking that you have understood

Note how Lorna checks that she has understood the information:

'Sorry, did you say there is an OAP discount?'

Some other expressions for checking information that the speaker may have already given:

When did you say it opened?

When did you say it shuts again?

I can't remember if you mentioned the seasonal times.

Can you remind me if concessions are available?

Sorry, how much does it cost to get in?

Sorry, I've forgotten how to get to the café / main entrance / ticket office.

2 For detailed comprehension of the vocabulary used, listen again and complete the gaps.

1 It costs .... for an adult.

2 A .... costs £6.

3 Are there .... for people in wheelchairs?

4 There is .... for people in wheelchairs.

5 Some of the access would be ....

6 Your grandmother .... to explore the entire reserve.

7 Did you say there is an OAP ....?

8 Members are allowed .... and OAPs can come in for £2.

Clear usage: polite language

Note some of the very polite language used by the speakers in this dialogue:

'*I was wondering* if you could help me.'

'*I'm planning* on coming to the farm, possibly this weekend.'

'*Could you tell me* ...?'

'*I'd like to know* the opening times and ...'

'*Would it be okay?*'

'*Would we be able to* walk around a bit with her?'

'If she could come, *that would be great.*'

3 Match the words on the left with the words which have similar meanings on the right.

1 a trail   a a charge / a fee

2 a reserve   b a protected area of land

3 facilities   c a route

4 a price   d resources

COBUILD CHECK: tourist attractions

- We offer **discounts** to children and **senior citizens**.
- Tickets are $46, with **concessions** and group bookings available.
- There are **special rates** for multiple bookings: if you book two or more places at the same time, you can claim a 10 per cent discount off the total bill.

FURTHER LISTENING

Listen to the recordings again and read through the transcripts. There are further recordings of Jessica, the Cape Town tourism representative in this book and on the website **www.collinselt.com/listening**.

7 HOTEL INFORMATION

BEFORE YOU LISTEN

This unit features two parts of a conversation covering an enquiry about room availability and directions.

- Do you often stay in hotels, guest houses, bed and breakfasts (B&Bs), or hostels?
- What do you look for when choosing where to stay?
- Do you always require certain facilities (e.g. air conditioning or a very quiet room) or are you relaxed about the accommodation you choose?

Note that unit 8 develops from this unit and covers practical matters concerned with checking in to a hotel and changing rooms.

A A potential guest from Los Angeles, Jeremy, phones the Tabard Inn in Washington, DC, to enquire about room availability.

1 Read the general comprehension questions below, then play the recording through once and answer the questions. The caller is from Los Angeles in the USA.

1 Which number on his telephone keypad did the caller press?
2 When does the caller plan to arrive at the hotel?
3 How much do the rooms with a queen-sized bed cost?
4 Where is the penthouse suite situated in the hotel?
5 What is the caller's reason for visiting the hotel?

Clear usage: informal language

In this conversation, Jeremy uses some very informal language:

'Do you guys have any suites available?'

'Do you guys have adjoining rooms?'

'I kinda wanna know the different options I've got available.'

It is often perfectly acceptable to use this type of language, but there are many circumstances in which you might wish to use more formal alternatives, just in case. More formal alternatives would be:

Do you have any suites available?

Could you tell me if you have any adjoining rooms?

I'd like to know the different options that are available.

Useful vocabulary and phrases: everyday hotel vocabulary

Check that you are familiar with the following words and phrases and refer to the mini-dictionary on page 84 as necessary. You will hear many of them used in this unit and also in unit 8. Are there other words and phrases that you would like to add to this list?

Room types

king-sized / queen-sized bed

double / single bed

suite

en suite

Room contents

towels

dressing gown

toiletries: soap, toothbrush, razor, comb, hairbrush, shampoo, conditioner

sewing kit

shoe-cleaning kit

safe

ironing board

trouser press

kettle and mugs

blanket

extra pillows

air conditioning (air-con)

Eating

restaurant opening times

continental breakfast

full English breakfast

buffet lunch

evening meal

half-board

full-board

Preferences

a terrace

a balcony

adjoining rooms

windows that open

away from traffic noise

a high / low floor

near / away from the lift / elevator

a room with a (sea / mountain) view

a quiet room at the back

a room overlooking the harbour

Note how Jeremy uses the word 'guys'. In American English, 'guys' is used to informally refer to 'all' (meaning boys, men, girls, and women). In most countries outside the USA, however, 'guys' is still mainly used to refer to men and boys.

---

2 **Now listen and fill in the key information that the receptionist provides. Pause or replay the recording when necessary.**

1 What would the .... be for that?

2 Okay, twenty-third to the ....

3 The starting rate is ....

4 Larger rooms .... are one ninety-five.

5 .... breakfast is included with all those.

6 The rooms get larger, there's more of a .... in each of the categories.

7 That has a king bed and a small .... area.

8 One of them has two double beds and it .... to a smaller room.

Clear usage: use of 'did' for emphasis in conditional sentences

Notice how Jeremy mentions *the possibility* that he might bring his girlfriend with him:

'If I did decide to bring my girlfriend with me … do you guys have any suites available?'

He uses the more emphatic 'did decide' rather than 'decided' in this question.

Other examples of this:

If we hired / did hire a car, how long would it take / does it take to drive to the hotel?

If I ordered / did order a continental breakfast, would it be included / is it included in the room price?

3 The questions on the left relate to fixed arrangements. Rewrite them so that they relate to 'tentative' or possible arrangements:

Example: When are you arriving?   *When would you be arriving?*

1   When are you leaving?   ....

2   Are you hiring a car?   ....

3   How are you going to pay the bill?   ....

4   Do you want a double room?   ....

5   Do you require a family room?   ....

The American hotel receptionist says: 'The starting rate is one sixty-five' by which he means $165.

This is a common way of expressing numbers in the USA. Other ways of expressing the same number:

one hundred and sixty-five dollars

one six five dollars

Note that in the UK, one sixty-five could be interpreted as $1.65, although common sense would indicate that a hotel room would not be so cheap.

B   In this second part of the conversation between Jeremy and the hotel receptionist, Jeremy asks about the best way to get to the hotel from the airport.

1   Play the recording through once. Are these statements true or false?

		True	False
1	Reagan National Airport is the nearest airport to the hotel.		
2	There are two other airports which Jeremy can fly into.		
3	You can take a subway train from Baltimore-Washington Airport.		
4	The Tabard Inn is located close to a subway station.		
5	The Tabard Inn is right next to the White House.		

Dupont Circle is a lively and cosmopolitan area of Washington, DC, to the north of downtown (i.e. central) Washington. Many art galleries, museums, embassies, and restaurants can be found there.

'subway' = metro. Both terms are used in the recording.

Washington, DC is often referred to simply as 'DC'.

2 **Now listen again. Complete the phrases to check your detailed comprehension.**

1 Reagan National is the .... You can take the metro— the subway.

2 Dulles is .... and a cab is probably the easiest.

3 It's about .... in a cab.

4 Baltimore-Washington Airport connects to a .... that you can take.

5 The metro is right .... so that gets you pretty much anywhere else you need to go.

6 Okay, that sounds great and .... know.

3 **Both speakers used a variety of phrases to establish a friendly tone to the telephone call. Listen to the recording again and underline the phrases you hear the speakers using.**

I'd be grateful for any advice you can give me.

Do you have any advice...?

That's great.

Okay, cool.

That's excellent.

That sounds good.

That sounds great.

Thank you very much.

Many thanks.

Have a good day.

Yeah, you too.

COBUILD CHECK: getting in from the airport

- **Take a cab** from the airport to the hotel.
- Middletown is a short **commuter train** ride south of Manhattan.
- The regular airport **shuttle bus** to the town centre takes about twenty minutes and costs £2.25 each way.
- When I arrived, I took the **subway** from the airport to the city centre.
- The whole of Ibiza can easily be reached from here using local buses from Ibiza town, the **transport hub**.

FURTHER LISTENING

Listen to the recordings again and read through the transcripts. There are many sources of 'authentic' recordings available on the Internet. For some video examples of speakers from around the world, go to the website **www.languagebyvideo.com**.

8 STAYING IN A HOTEL

BEFORE YOU LISTEN

This unit focuses on arriving at and booking into a hotel and then requesting a change of room.

- Do you have any special preferences when you stay in a hotel, hostel, or guest house – a room on a high floor, away from the lift, or with a good view?
- Have you often needed to change your hotel room? Why?
- Do you find it easy to complain if you receive poor service?
- Do you tend to be quite polite when you complain or can you be quite aggressive?

A **In the first recording, Nikki, who is from Edinburgh in Scotland, arrives at a hotel in Melbourne, Australia.**

1 **Play the recording through once. Are these statements true or false?**

	True	False
1 Nikki already has a room reservation.		
2 She would like a single en-suite room.		
3 She decides to pay with a credit card.		
4 She would like the opportunity to charge dinner, drinks, etc. to her room bill.		
5 She is given a room on the fourth floor.		

The receptionist says:

'If you wish to charge anything back to the room, i.e. any room service, dinner or drinks ...'

He uses the abbreviation 'i.e.' (originally from the Latin *id est,* meaning 'that is'). He could also have said 'e.g.' (originally from the Latin *examplia gratia*, meaning 'for example'):

If you wish to charge anything back to the room, e.g. any room service, dinner or drinks ...

These terms are rarely used in spoken English but are very common in written contexts.

---

2 **Now listen again to the recording and complete the phrases.**

1   I'll ………………… that for you, madam.

2   Yes, we do have ………………… for you this evening.

3   Yes, it does have an …………………. .

4   It also has an English breakfast ………………… in the rate.

5   What I'll need from you, madam, is just ………………… and also if you'd like to pay cash or card.

6   Okay, madam, so that's ……………………………………, with breakfast included …

7   Would you like me to …………………………………… in the room for you?

8   I'll just be …………………………………… just for the room cost.

9   But if you wish to order any …………………, I'll take an additional $50.

10 Okay, thank you, madam. That's …………………………………… you now.

Useful vocabulary and phrases: checking into a hotel

I have a reservation in the name of Spiller.

Do you need my passport?

I'd like a quiet room away from the lifts / on the ground floor.

Does the room have a bath / a shower / free Wi-Fi / air conditioning?

I'd prefer a room with a bath, if possible.

Can I see the room, please?

Is it possible to upgrade the room?

Could you put an extra bed / a fan / an ironing board in the room?

What time do you serve dinner?

Do you offer late check-out?

Can we have a wake-up call, please?

Can I keep my room until 2 pm?

I'll need to swipe your credit card.

Clear usage: checking wishes and requests

The receptionist has to find out which hotel services the guest requires. He offers lots of options using the following structure:

'*If you wish* to charge anything back to the room …'

'But *if you wish* to order any room service …'

This language is quite formal. Here are some less formal, but still polite, alternatives:

If you want / need to charge anything back to the room …

If you would like to order any room service …

COBUILD CHECK: hotel check-in

- Prices, **availability**, and reservations can all be confirmed in just one call.
- When you reach your rooms, your **luggage** will already be there.
- A **porter** carried their luggage upstairs to a three-room suite.
- Guests must present their passports at the hotel **check-in desk** on arrival.
- We **checked in** and were shown to a room on the third floor.
- When we **checked out** of our hotel, the bill featured items we had not consumed.

3 Now listen for the language Nikki uses in response to the information given by the hotel receptionist. Underline the phrases you hear Nikki use. All of them are appropriate phrases, but not all of them are used in this dialogue.

Sorry, could you repeat that?

Did you say $50 per night?

Okay, so $250 per night?

I'll probably want to go with that.

Wonderful.

That sounds good.

What does that mean?

That would be great.

Sorry, I don't understand.

Fantastic.

Excellent.

That's good to hear.

Great, thank you.

That's great. Many thanks.

Perfect.

I'm not sure about that.

B   In this recording, Nikki goes to Reception to sort out some problems with her room.

1 Play the recording through once. Then decide which one of these statements best describes the outcome of Nikki's conversation with the receptionist.

	True	False
1 She is happy to stay in her original room if the air conditioning is fixed.		
2 She needs earplugs to help her sleep.		
3 She is going to move to another, quieter room on the fourth floor.		
4 She is going to move to another room on a different, quieter floor.		

2 Now listen again and fill in the gaps. The focus of this exercise is on the very polite and obliging language used by the guest to make her requests.

1   Actually there's …….. with my room.

2   So I ….................... you could ….................... get somebody to have a look at it for me?

3   I have to admit it's …..................... quite a noisy room.

4   I …..................... there's any chance of me moving rooms, …......................?

5   I'm quite a light sleeper, so …..................... not having to worry about the noise outside.

6   No, that's it. ……...........................…................... for your help.

Clear usage: 'seem'

'The air conditioning doesn't *seem* to be working.'

Nikki uses the verb *seem* as she does not want to appear to be totally confident in her complaint to the receptionist. By using such language she wants to leave open the possibility that she may simply not have understood the air conditioning controls!

Other examples of tentative language:

There seems to be a problem with the shower.

There doesn't seem to be any soap in the room.

The water doesn't seem to be running out of the tap.

Here is a more direct approach:

It isn't working.   The shower is broken.   There isn't any soap.   There is no water!

3 **Complete the sentences by matching the words and phrases from the column on the left with those from the column on the right.**

1	I've organized an internal room	a	that much stuff with me.
2	I can send up	b	which faces the courtyard.
3	Then there won't	c	your new keys to the room.
4	I don't have	d	maintenance in the next 10–15 minutes.
5	Here are	e	be any road noise.

COBUILD CHECK: hotel rooms – locations

- The windows of the room **overlooked** a small courtyard shaded by a palm tree.
- Be sure to ask for a room with a **harbour** view.
- She led us to a room with a **balcony** overlooking the harbour.
- We went to a room at the **end of the corridor**.
- The guests complained about the **street noise**, particularly from cars with loud stereos and motorcycles with loud exhausts.
- People who like meditation prefer rooms **at the back of the hotel**.

FURTHER LISTENING

Listen to the recordings again and read through the transcripts. For further recordings, including a recording of Nikki asking for some directions from the hotel, go to the website, **www.collinselt.com/listening**.

9 PHONE TRANSACTIONS

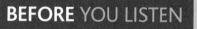

BEFORE YOU LISTEN

These two recordings feature two phone transactions: one is a person-to-person call and the other is to an automated voice recognition system.

- What has been your experience of dealing with automated phone systems?
- Do they irritate you or do you find that they are efficient?
- Would you rather talk to a person or a machine?

A The first recording in this unit features the automated booking and information service for the Vue cinema chain in the UK. What kind of questions would you expect the service to ask you, if you wanted to buy tickets for a film?

1 Play the recording through once. Are these statements true or false?

	True	False
1 The film chosen, *Tree of Life*, has only one further performance on the day the caller enquires.		
2 The running time of the film is a hundred and forty-nine minutes.		
3 If you need to book for a large group, you need to press the hash key.		
4 There is only availability at the back of the auditorium.		

Certificate 12a

The film *Tree of Life* is a 'certificate 12a' in the UK, which means that it is only recommended for children who are over the age of 12 and are accompanied by an adult.

Useful vocabulary and phrases: automated phone systems

hash key	Please key in your card number followed by hash.
star key	
Press one, two, three, *etc.*	Please stay on the line.
Please wait while we connect you.	Thank you for waiting.
Please wait while we transfer you.	Thank you for your patience.

2 Check your understanding of key information. Listen again, stop the recording as necessary and complete the gaps in the sentences.

1 Welcome to the .... Vue booking and information line.

2 The remaining .... for today is 6.10 pm.

3 To book tickets or hear ...., just stay on the line.

4 How many tickets do you need ....?

5 We have .... and VIP seats. Which would you prefer?

6 So the total cost will be ....

7 Remember you'll need to bring .... with you when you come to collect your tickets.

8 Right, please key in your card number, followed by the ....

COBUILD CHECK: processing bookings

- **Advance booking** is highly recommended.
- Air Canada advises people not to go to the airport unless they have a **confirmed booking**.
- When he tried to cancel the booking, he was told that a £150 **cancellation fee** would be deducted from his refund.
- Book online or telephone the credit card booking line: 020 1321 2233 (**transaction fee** of £1 per ticket).
- This includes a **credit card handling fee** of £2.50.
- They will be able to choose a date and time for their appointment from a variety of **options**.

Clear usage: the imperative, the present perfect, and 'will' in bookings

Note the following three patterns used by the automated service.

The imperative form, used to give instructions on how to use the service:

'*Say* the name of the film.'

'*Stay* on the line.'

'Please *wait* while I check availability for you.'

The present perfect, used to confirm information:

'*You've chosen Tree of Life.*' (*active form*)

'Those tickets *have been reserved*.' (*passive form*)

Will is used to give further information:

'So the total cost *will be* twenty pounds, seventy.'

'Remember, *you'll need to* bring your card with you when you come to collect your tickets.'

Another example would be:

You will need to be at the cinema five minutes before the performance starts.

3 Match the nouns taken from the recording (on the left) with words that have similar meanings (on the right).

1 performance   **a** charge
2 running time   **b** showing
3 booking   **c** alternative
4 fee   **d** reservation
5 auditorium   **e** duration
6 option   **f** chairs
7 seating   **g** theatre

B In this first extract from a call to a UK-based car rental company, Jack, the car rental assistant, is giving Mr Chick a quotation for hiring a car to drive from San Francisco to Las Vegas.

1 Play the recording through once. Are these statements true or false? Before listening, you may want to familiarize yourself with some of the specific terms relating to car hire (such as 'collision damage waiver'), which can be found in the mini-dictionary on page 84.

	True	False

1 Mr Chick's wife will also be driving the car.
2 Jack suggests a car that will be suitable for four people.
3 Jack guarantees that the car will be a Hyundai Sonata.
4 There will be no charge for mileage.
5 The package quoted includes a free tank of petrol.
6 Mr Chick is surprised by the low price he is quoted for the car hire.

2 Now listen again and complete the phrases below. If there are any car hire terms you are unfamiliar with, use the mini-dictionary to help you.

1 Taking ………………….. that your wife wants to drive as well.
2 I'm going to suggest to you an …………………..-class vehicle.
3 Four doors, automatic transmission, with ………………….. .
4 This specific vehicle will come with ………………….. mileage on there.
5 In addition to that, you've also got ………………….. that consists of …………………..
    damage waiver …
6 ………………….. protection, third-party liability insurance.
7 Those are the three components that make up a ………………….. policy.
8 In addition to that, you're also getting ………………….. liability insurance.
9 Those have all got a zero ………………….. on them, okay?
10 I'm going to quote you on a package which also includes the initial ………………….. of
    fuel.

Clear usage: 'pick up' and 'drop off'

Note that Mr Chick will *pick up* the car in San Francisco and *drop it off* in Las Vegas.

Some other uses of these verbs:

I'll pick you up at 8 o'clock.

Could you pick me up a little earlier?

Where would you like me to drop you off?

I'll drop you off at the end of the road.

I share the school run with another mother – I drop the kids off in the morning and she picks them up in the afternoon.

3 Match the words which are used in the recording (on the left) with the words that, in this context, have similar meanings (on the right).

1	vehicle	**a**	full
2	mileage	**b**	length
3	insurance	**c**	part
4	collision	**d**	stealing
5	comprehensive	**e**	cover
6	theft	**f**	responsibility
7	liability	**g**	crash
8	component	**h**	first
9	initial	**i**	distance
10	duration	**j**	car

COBUILD CHECK: inclusive features

- Specific Saturday delivery can be arranged **at no extra charge**.
- You'll also have **unlimited** access to the swimming pool and gym.
- It **comes with** unlimited mileage and insurance.
- Insurance is included **as part of the package**.
- The **package includes** a phone and twelve months' line rental.

FURTHER LISTENING

Listen to the recordings again and read through the transcripts. For further extracts from these recordings, including the request for a car hire quotation and a discussion of the confirmation procedure, go to **www.collinselt.com/listening**.

10 FACE-TO-FACE TRANSACTIONS

BEFORE YOU LISTEN

This unit contains two recordings, one in a mobile phone shop and the other in a currency exchange office. In both cases, the client needs to understand exactly what he is being told by the salesman / agent to ensure a successful transaction.

- How do you check politely that you have understood what has been said?
- How do you ask someone to repeat information?
- How do you indicate that you are listening carefully?
- Have you changed money when abroad?
- Do you go to the bank / currency exchange office or do you prefer to use cash machines?

A In this recording, a customer visits a mobile phone shop to enquire about new phones. Both speakers are from London, but listen out for differences in their accents. You may want to check the phone-specific vocabulary in the mini-dictionary and in Exercise 2 *before* doing Exercise 1.

1 Read the questions below. Then play the recording and answer the questions to test your general comprehension of the conversation.

1 Why is the customer looking for a new mobile phone?
2 Does the customer require a 'touch-screen' phone?
3 How many phones does the salesman show the customer?
4 How much will the new contract cost per month?

Qwerty keypad

The traditional English-language layout for a computer keyboard is the *qwerty* set-up. This name comes from the letters which appear in the top left row of the English-language keyboard: Q-W-E-R-T-Y.

---

2 Now listen again and complete the phrases.

1 The contract on my current phone .... pretty soon and I'd like to upgrade.
2 Are you after like a .... phone or a qwerty-keypad phone?
3 My current phone isn't particularly ....

4   I mean it's quite .... It's got Wi-Fi, it's got GPS ...
5   You can .... all sorts of different apps.
6   So if you're not too .... with, for example, touch-screen phones ...
7   Some people just .... to use a qwerty keypad and similar function[s].
8   Both phones are quite good and .... as well.

Clear usage: expressing preferences

Note the customer's way of telling the salesman what he requires in response to the question, 'What kind of phone are you after?':

'I *definitely want* a phone that has the Internet.'
'*I'm not really sure* about [...] a touch-screen phone.'
'*I think I'd find* the touch-screen quite hard to use.'

Other useful expressions:
I'd prefer to have a very light phone.
I'm not keen on phones with too many functions.
I need something that can take good photos.

3 **Complete the gaps. Choose words from the box.**

1   These phones have a lot of ...... high-tech ...... features.
2   My phone .... runs out next month.
3   The .... feature is very useful. It means I always know where I am.
4   I spend a lot of time on Facebook™ but I don't use ....
5   I prefer having a .... keypad because you can type faster that way.
6   I can't get used to texting on a .... phone.
7   My phone is very old – I need to .... it.

contract

qwerty

touch-screen

GPS

~~high-tech~~

Twitter™

upgrade

COBUILD CHECK: phone applications

- The more **apps** that are available for the phone, the more attractive it will become to prospective purchasers.
- I'd say I delete about 90 per cent of free apps a day after I **download** them.
- Developers can directly **upload** their apps along with the price for them.
- The application uses the phone's built-in **GPS** to show users things to do near them, covering bars, restaurants, theatres, cinemas, and cafés.
- I worked around the problem by **installing** the app on a memory card.
- The company's **free app** is simple, but potentially useful.

B This recording concerns a face-to-face dialogue in a currency exchange office.

1 Read the statements below and then play the recording. Check your general comprehension by indicating whether the statements are true or false.

	True	False
1 The customer will be visiting two countries.		
2 She wants to exchange the same amount of currency for each of her trips.		
3 She is advised that it would be better to buy the dollars at a later date.		
4 The agent recommends taking currency in smaller denominations to Spain.		
5 The customer decides to only take small denominations in US dollars as well.		

2 Now listen again and this time pay particular attention to the way the customer actively listens to the agent and keeps the discussion flowing. Fill in the language used by the traveller in the latter part of the dialogue. Note the use of words such as *yeah*, *right*, and *okay*, and of questions and repetition.

Agent: I can give you four hundred and forty euros, for four hundred pounds.

Customer: Okay. **1** .... As I'm going to ...

[...]

Agent: ... At the moment [it's] the best time to buy.

Customer: **2** ....
Okay, thanks. ... Okay, well, I'd like to go ahead ...

[...]

Agent: ... They rather prefer small denominations in Spain, yeah?

Customer: **3** .... Thank you.

Agent: And what about US dollars? You want the small denominations as well for that?

Customer: Um, **4** .... fine.

Agent: ... That's fine. ... We can give you some twenties, tens, fives, and one dollar ...

Customer: Yeah, so, maybe two one-hundred dollar bills? **5** ....

Useful vocabulary and phrases: changing money

How many dollars are there to the yen?

What is the current rate of the euro against the yuan?

I'd like two twenties and the rest in tens.

Do you take a commission?

Can I return any unused currency?

UK currency: five- / ten- / twenty- / fifty-pound notes; fifty- / ten- / five-pence coins

US currency: notes [*UK*] = bills [*US*]; nickel = five cents; dime = ten cents; quarter = 25 cents

COBUILD CHECK: foreign currency

- The typical bill for withdrawing £500 from an **ATM** abroad will be about £25.
- Many people use their ATM card abroad to buy **foreign currency** but the facility is not available in all countries.
- If you are going to an exotic location, where you are unsure about the **local currency**, you can call us any time for advice.
- Photocopy **high denomination** banknotes so that you have a record of the serial numbers.
- They still use paper notes for even **low denominations** like one dollar.

Clear usage: advice, recommendations, and requests

Note the language used in the dialogue for giving advice and making requests:

Advice / recommendations

'You need to take US dollars.'

'I can give you six hundred and forty-two dollars. Yeah?'

'I would recommend [that you] take some smaller denominations. Let's say fifties and below.'

'We [could] give you some twenties, tens, fives, and one dollar ...'

Requests

'I would like to buy some currency, please.'

'Could I have, maybe, four hundred pounds?'

'Is it best for me to buy the US dollars now?'

'What denominations can I have?'

3 In each set of three words below, two have similar meanings. Underline the odd one out.

1 currency	notes	bills
2 convert	deliver	exchange
3 agent	clerk	customer
4 sell	buy	purchase
5 deal	transaction	meeting
6 bank	ATM	cash machine

FURTHER LISTENING

Listen to the recordings again and read through the transcripts. For further recordings, go to **www.collinselt.com/listening**.

11 ANNOUNCEMENTS

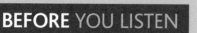

This unit features recordings of announcements – at a theatre / cinema complex, at a station, and on the radio.

- Have you ever had problems understanding announcements – at a train station or airport, for example?
- If so, what happened? Did you miss the train? Did you go to the wrong platform / gate?

A In the first recording, you will hear five short announcements about events at Riverside Studios theatre and cinema complex in west London.

1 Play the five short announcements through once. Then answer the questions below, one for each announcement, to check your general understanding.

1 Where is the film, *Pan's Labyrinth*, being shown?
2 If you are going to studio 2, what must you do now?
3 When will the performance of *The City Weeps* start?
4 This is the 'final call' for which film?
5 This announcement is directed to ladies, gentlemen, and who else?

The *Tête-à-Tête* opera festival, which ran at Riverside Studios in the summer of 2011, was designed as 'a festival for opera fans with open minds, patience, a sense of humour, and no preconceptions'.

COBUILD CHECK: at the theatre

- Mobile phones must be **switched off** at all times.
- Ladies and gentlemen, please **take your seats** for the concert.
- Tonight's **performance** is conducted by Marc Minkowski.
- Cries of 'bravo' and ten minutes of rapturous **applause** heralded yesterday's opening performance as a resounding success.
- When he finished the song, there was a **standing ovation**.
- The **box office** queue began to form twenty-four hours in advance of the opening.

2 **Now listen again to the five announcements. Stop the recording as necessary and complete the gaps in the sentences to check your detailed comprehension.**

1 The cinema's ….................. for tonight's film, *Pan's Labyrinth* …

2 … starting ….................., please …

3 This is ….................. please for tonight's performance in studio 2.

4 ….................. to switch off your mobiles and take your seats.

5 Welcome to *Tête-à-Tête*, the ….................. festival.

6 Studio ….................. is now open for tonight's performance of *The City Weeps*.

7 This is a final call for tonight's film, *X-Men: First Class*, ….................. to start.

8 Please could you ….................. . This is a final call.

9 This morning's performance by Hairy Maclary ….................. in five minutes.

10 Please could you take your seats. This is a ….................. call.

Clear usage: some expressions of future time

The announcer says that the performances will start *in five minutes* or that they are *just about to* start.

Some other expressions of future time to listen out for:

in a couple of minutes	*just after 4.30*
in ten minutes / two hours	*some time soon*
later this morning	*immediately*
just before 3 o'clock	*shortly*

Useful vocabulary and phrases: railways, platforms, and trains

mind the gap	the train is about to depart
move along the platform	escalator
stand behind the yellow lines	lift
let the passengers off	ticket office
move along the train / along the carriage	ticket barriers
stand clear of the door	tickets and travel cards

After you listen

The two films mentioned in the recording were *Pan's Labyrinth* and *X-Men: First Class*.

- Have you seen either of these films?
- What kinds of films do you enjoy watching?
- Do you prefer going to the cinema or watching movies at home?

B Naeem Mohammed is from Huddersfield, a town in Yorkshire in the north of England, but he now lives in London. In this recording you will listen to five announcements that he makes for passengers travelling on the London Underground.

1 Play the recording through once. For each of the recordings, identify which statement is correct.

1 a The train approaching the platform is a non-stop train to Heathrow Airport.
   b The train approaching the platform will call at all stations to Heathrow Airport.

2 a The next station for the next train is Ealing Broadway.
   b The next train will stop at other stations before reaching Ealing Broadway.

3 a The next train to Richmond will be in two minutes.
   b The next train to Richmond will be in four minutes.

4 a You must not stand near the platform exits and entrances.
   b You should stay near the platform exits and entrances.

5 a You should get on the train as quickly as possible.
   b You should wait until passengers have gotten off the train before you get on.

2 Now listen again. Complete the phrases. Focus on the key terms Naeem uses in his announcements.

1 This train .... at Acton Town. When this train .... the platform, please make sure …

2 Let the passengers off the train first before .... and .... between the train and the platform.

3 Please make sure you stand behind the .... at all times.

4 Ladies and gentlemen, you .... to use the whole area of the platform. Keep away from the exit and ....

5 Your next train on platform two is your .... Piccadilly line.

> Do you find any aspects of Naeem's pronunciation unfamiliar, e.g. the final sound in *calling, approaching*, and *boarding*? He leaves off the 'g' and says *callin'*. This is common in many regional English accents.

COBUILD CHECK: transport announcements

- Please **stand clear** of the doors.
- Once again, it's time to remind passengers to **stand away from** the doors.
- Passengers are reminded to keep their personal luggage with them **at all times**.
- While we're waiting to be cleared for takeoff, I'd like to take this opportunity to review the **safety procedures** for this flight.
- **Allowing other passengers to get off** makes it easier for you to get on and quickly find a seat.
- **Stand back** from the door.

③ Match the words and phrases from the recording (on the left) with those with similar meanings (on the right).

1	mind	a	stop at
2	board	b	be careful about
3	alight	c	get on
4	call at	d	go up
5	ascend	e	go down
6	descend	f	get off

C In the final recording you will hear a weather forecast from radio station 3AW, based in Melbourne, Australia.

① Read the statements below and then play the recording through once. Are the statements true or false?

	True	False
1 Today is mainly going to be sunny.		
2 It is going to rain during the day tomorrow.		
3 The wind is going to get stronger later.		
4 Waves will be up to one and a half metres.		

A *knot* (note the pronunciation, *not*) = 1 nautical mile per hour = exactly 1.852 kilometres per hour and approximately 1.151 miles per hour

In Australia and most of the world, people use degrees Celsius (°C) to measure temperature. In the USA and its territories (such as Puerto Rico and Guam), degrees Fahrenheit (°F) is used instead.

Melbourne, Australia

The weather forecast on track 24 is for the city of Melbourne, in the south-east of Australia. Melbourne is the second most densely-populated city in Australia and is the capital of the state of Victoria.

'Sydenham' and 'Boronia' are suburbs of Melbourne.

The forecaster talks about 'The Bays'. To the south of Melbourne, there are many bays and beaches which are sometimes collectively referred to as The Bays.

To find Melbourne on a map, go to **www.collinsmaps.com** and search for 'Melbourne'.

FURTHER LISTENING

Listen to the recordings again and read through the transcripts. Go to the website **www.collinselt.com/listening**. Record the announcements you need to understand – perhaps on your phone if you can. Then listen back to them carefully. The more times you listen, the easier the announcements will become to understand in the future.

12 SCHOOL DAYS

BEFORE YOU LISTEN

The first speaker briefly describes the UK school system in general, the second speaker describes his experiences of being at boarding school, and the final speaker, now a teacher, reflects on her experience of school life.

- How would you describe the school system in your country?
- Did you enjoy your school days?
- What is your opinion of children 'going away' to boarding school?
- What would you expect the second speaker to say about his experience of boarding school?

A Lisa, a recent UK university graduate, explains a little about the school system in the UK.

1 Read the general comprehension questions below. Then play the recording through once. Can you answer the questions?

1 When do you start primary school in the UK?
2 According to Lisa, when does compulsory education end?
3 What is the alternative to staying at high school for sixth form?
4 When did Lisa leave her high school?
5 Do all the countries in the UK (England, Scotland, Wales, and Northern Ireland) share the same system of education?

The 'sixth form' which Lisa refers to covers the final two years of academic education in English, Welsh, and Northern Irish schools (from the age of 16 to 18, usually).

Lisa uses the term 'high school' but you may hear 'secondary school' used too. They mean the same thing.

Clear usage: word order for emphasis

Lisa says:

'Usually, you attend' rather than the more common form: *You usually attend*. Placing words such as *usually, sometimes, occasionally*, and *often* at the front of the sentence adds emphasis to the statement.

COBUILD CHECK: stages of education

- She was introduced to books by her **kindergarten** teacher.
- All children receive a **primary education**, many beginning before the age of five.
- In **elementary school**, I was really shy.
- The policy applies to students in Grade 1 through **senior high school**.
- The **sixth form**, which comprised two years of instruction, was taught in small sets of eight to ten students.

2 **Now listen again, stop the recording as necessary, and complete the gaps in the sentences, which represent key points to be understood. Lisa is from the north east of England. Are there any aspects of her accent that you find difficult to understand?**

1 If your school has a sixth form, ... to stay till you're eighteen.

2 Or you can go to college when .... and get the same qualifications.

3 A lot of schools .... don't have a sixth form.

4 Schools in Scotland are .... different.

5 In England and Wales, you go to school .... than you do in Scotland.

6 And then Northern Ireland has ...., so that's different ...

Clear usage: conditional forms

Note that Lisa says:

'I went to high school for seven years ... If I was in Scotland, I *would have gone* for six years and then gone to university.'

This form of the verb, known as the 'third conditional', indicates that the possibility of going to school for six years rather than seven no longer exists as she has already completed her school education. Compare with this sentence:

If I lived in Scotland, I would go to high school for six years.

In this case the speaker is of school age and therefore can talk about the possibility of attending school for six years if she *lived in* or *moved to* Scotland now.

B **You are going to listen to James who attended a boarding school in the south of England.**

1 **Read the general comprehension questions below. Then play the recording through once and answer the questions.**

1 Why did his parents not send him to day schools?

2 How long did James spend at boarding schools?

3 Did he enjoy his school days?

4 Did he prefer to visit his friends' parents' houses or stay in school at the weekends?

James went to a 'boarding school'. A boarding school is a school at which children live, sleep, eat, and study. The children go home to visit their families on weekends and in the holidays. Children that live at the school are called 'boarders'. Those who go home every day are called 'day pupils'.

'Prep' (preparatory) schools are usually independent schools that prepare pupils in the UK for the 'common entrance' exam which is taken at 14. These schools can be for boarders or day pupils.

2 Now listen again. Complete the phrases.

1 I went to ………………… from the age of seven.

2 So the best thing for me was to go and have ………………… at one school.

3 I was at a ………………… from seven till fourteen.

4 The main difference obviously to ………………… is that I was at school most of the time.

5 There were quite a few activities ………………… for us.

6 A lot of the boys ………………… to go home quite often.

7 That was quite good fun for ………………… who had parents living overseas.

8 You had the ………………… to yourself and all the teachers were sort of quietly ………………… business.

Clear usage: talking about past events and actions

James generally uses standard simple past forms to describe past events in his life, e.g.:

'I *went* to boarding school from the age of seven.'

'My parents *lived* in Germany at the time.'

'It *was* the logical thing to do.'

He emphasizes what his parents were doing for periods of their lives by using the continuous form of the past:

'They *were moving* around ...'

And note his use of *would* to describe regular occurrences in the past:

'I *would stay* there ...'

'We *would occasionally be let out* on the weekends.'

C In this recording, Laura compares her time as a student with her new life as a teacher.

1 Listen to the recording once. Are these statements true or false?

	True	False
1 She enjoys chatting with the older schoolchildren.		
2 She does not get angry when the children do not pay attention in class.		
3 She would rather be a teacher than a student.		
4 She now understands that being a teacher is hard work.		

2 **Now listen again and complete the gaps in the sentences to focus on some key vocabulary and grammar points.**

1 There's a sort of relationship where you almost want to, kind of, be more ……………… with them.

2 You've got to ……………… line.

3 I'm ……………… if they're not— you know, they're talking or if they're looking away.

4 I do remember school ……………… very tiring.

5 I wish it ……………… me that was at the desk.

6 ... writing things down. ………………, you know, being the teacher is just so much work.

7 So I kind of now ……………… some of the teachers that I had, if that makes sense.

Clear usage: 'remember'

Note the way Laura forms a sentence with *remember* when she has a memory of something happening in the past:

'I *do* remember school *being* very tiring'.

Other examples:

I *remember it being* difficult.

I *remember leaving my phone* on the school bus once.

I *remember having to work* very hard.

Compare this with the use of *remember* when you need to remember to do something in the future:

I *must* **remember to take** my book back to the library.

I *must* **remember to call** John later.

---

3 **Match the adjectives on the left with those with similar meanings on the right.**

1	chatty	a	odd
2	tiring	b	angry
3	strange	c	exhausting
4	annoyed	d	grateful
5	tired	e	talkative
6	appreciative	f	exhausted

FURTHER LISTENING

Listen to the recordings again and read through the transcripts. For further recordings of Lisa and James, go to the website **www.collinselt.com/listening**.

13 PREPARING FOR WORK

In the first two recordings in this unit, you will hear speakers talking about their experience of university life. In the third recording, the speaker talks about finding a first job.

- How would you describe the system of higher education in your country?
- At what age do you normally leave school, college, or university in your country?
- How would you describe your experience of education since leaving school (if you have left school)?

A Lisa, who spoke about school-level education in the previous unit, now talks about universities. She starts by saying that she thinks UK universities have a different focus to universities in other countries. What do you think this 'different focus' might be? What do you consider the main focus of your education to be / to have been?

1 Play the recording through once. Are these statements true or false?

	True	False
1 You are often given a lot of free time at UK universities.		
2 The stereotypical student wastes a lot of time sleeping, going out, etc.		
3 Lisa was the social secretary for the university ski club.		
4 Her student loan meant that she had plenty of money to spend on clothes, etc.		

> Lisa often uses the common UK slang 'uni', to mean 'university'. Note that uni is also used in Australia, but is not the standard slang term for university worldwide. For example, in South Africa, 'varsity' is used while in the USA, university is regularly referred to as 'college' or simply as 'school'.

> Lisa talks about her 'student loan'. Student loans in the UK are taken out to cover university / college fees and accommodation costs. The loan is repaid once the student begins to earn a salary which exceeds a certain amount.

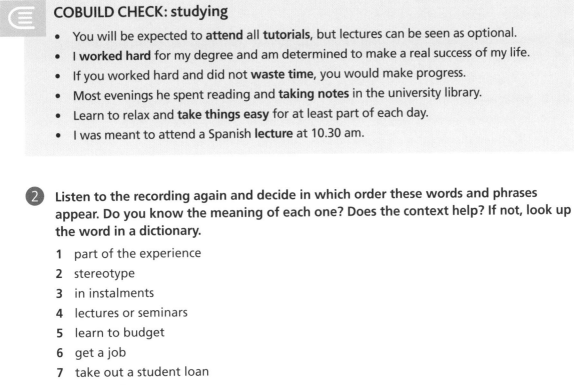

COBUILD CHECK: studying

- You will be expected to **attend** all **tutorials**, but lectures can be seen as optional.
- I **worked hard** for my degree and am determined to make a real success of my life.
- If you worked hard and did not **waste time**, you would make progress.
- Most evenings he spent reading and **taking notes** in the university library.
- Learn to relax and **take things easy** for at least part of each day.
- I was meant to attend a Spanish **lecture** at 10.30 am.

2 Listen to the recording again and decide in which order these words and phrases appear. Do you know the meaning of each one? Does the context help? If not, look up the word in a dictionary.

1 part of the experience
2 stereotype
3 in instalments
4 lectures or seminars
5 learn to budget
6 get a job
7 take out a student loan
8 temptation   ....

3 Which words in the recording have similar meanings to the following? You may want to refer to the transcript to do this exercise.

1 a schedule   ....
2 a very strong attraction ....
3 payments   ....
4 very large   ....
5 to plan your spending   ....
6 spare   ....

After you listen

- What is your impression of Lisa's university experience?
- Did she enjoy it?
- Do you think she used her time well?
- Was she able to live on her student loan or was she complaining about having a lack of money while she was at university?
- How does Lisa's explanation of the UK university system differ to the system where you're from? Can you think of some positives and negatives of both systems?

B The next speaker, Grant, summarizes his university experience, from his first degree through to studying for a PhD.

1 Read the general comprehension question below. Then play the recording through once and answer each question.

1 What did Grant study for his undergraduate degree?
2 What was the most important aspect for him of doing his first degree?
3 In comparison, what was his attitude towards doing a Master's degree?
4 What was his career plan when he was studying for his PhD?

> Listen out for how Grant uses the phrase 'ended up': 'I somehow ended up doing Latin as well'. This implies that he did not necessarily have a great desire or determination to study his particular subjects, but almost 'fell into' studying them. See the mini-dictionary (pg 84) for a full definition of 'end up'.

2 Now listen again for key phrases which show how Grant felt about specific stages of his studies. Complete the phrases.

1 My undergraduate degree, it was very much about ………………….. It was about …
2 I studied English Literature. Somehow I ended up doing Latin as well which was ………………… my will.
3 I then went on to do a Masters at a different university, which was …………………. focused.
4 You were there because ……………………………………… there.
5 I was all ………………… a career as an academic. And then it all changed.

> Did you notice Grant's ironic comment about his degree in English literature being 'economically useful'. Did you hear in his tone of voice that he was being sarcastic? What is actually implied by his comment, then?

Clear usage: emphatic language

Note the language Grant uses to signal points that he wants to emphasize; note also the repetition of *all* in the last two statements:

'It was very much about the social side.'
'It was about leaving home for the first time.'
'You were there because you wanted to be there.'
'It was much more about the discipline.'
'So I was all—all set for a career in ...'
'And then it all— it all changed.'

C In the final recording for this unit, Jeremy, who is from Los Angeles in the USA, talks about the importance of preparing a good CV to get a job.

1 Play the recording through once. Which of the following statements does not represent Jeremy's thoughts about getting a job straight after university?

1 College graduates should stress how well they did at school / university.
2 College graduates have the experience that companies are looking for.
3 Employers ask for experience, even though new graduates do not have any.
4 You should persuade potential employers to value your qualities, even if you do not have experience.

Note that Jeremy says 'employee' when he means to say 'employer'. We all make occasional mistakes when we speak. In English, this is called a 'slip of the tongue'.

Jeremy also refers to 'college' and 'school' interchangeably, but could equally use 'university'. In the USA, all of these terms can be used to refer to university. However, in British English, only university (or uni) can be used.

2 Now listen again. Complete the phrases to check your detailed comprehension and check any unfamiliar words in the mini-dictionary.

1 When you're writing a CV or a ...., when you're doing it straight out of college.
2 What you .... is education, though.
3 That's the first thing that they need to put and make .... for.
4 Most of the experience you'll have isn't really gonna .... you.
5 ... which is kind of a .... for first-time workers.
6 Your .... is just convincing an [employer] to take a chance.

COBUILD CHECK: getting a job

• The beauty of a short **CV** is that it can easily be adapted to suit the job for which you are applying.
• I got a job **straight out of college** as a copywriter in a small recruitment ad agency.
• It is decidedly difficult to secure a good job, regardless of how **well educated** you are.
• The education details are of much greater relevance to the graduate, while **work experience** is of lesser importance.

FURTHER LISTENING

Listen to the recordings again and read through the transcripts. For further recordings of all the speakers in this unit, go to the website **www.collinselt.com/listening**.

14 WORKING LIFE

The speakers in this unit talk about their day-to-day work and some current projects.

- How would you describe your everyday work and routines?
- Do any of the jobs described in the recordings appeal to you?
- What would be your ideal job?

A The first speaker, John, is from the south of England. He is an HR (Human Resources) manager, the person responsible for personnel matters in an organization. What would you expect the everyday work of an HR manager to be?

1 Read the questions below, and then play the recording through once. Answer the questions to check your general understanding. Note that John uses quite a lot of 'business jargon'. How easy does he make it for the listener who is not familiar with his particular work?

1 Does John's job follow a regular daily pattern?
2 What is the first thing he does when he gets to work?
3 John is recruiting ten people for open job vacancies at the moment. True or false?
4 When will John be 'rolling out' (starting) the new online performance review?
5 Why is he so concerned about recruiting the right people for the vacant jobs?

2 Now listen again and reorder the following phrases. As you listen, focus on understanding the business jargon that John uses. Can you work out the meanings from the context? Check your understanding by referring to the mini-dictionary or to your own dictionary.

1 … making sure you don't **drop any balls** in the process.
2 I'm **devising a programme** that I can **roll out** next week.
3 We've **just launched** our online performance review.
4 I'm devising a training programme for our **performance reviews**.
5 … which will change, you know, **the whole landscape** of what you're gonna face.
6 I've got to make sure they're all **tracking on time**.
7 So that I can be **up to speed**.
8 It's all about **priorities and deadlines**.   ....

COBUILD CHECK: paying attention to detail

- It has been a few years of hard work and **meticulous** planning, but it has been well worth it.
- Throughout this investigation, we have been painstakingly **thorough**.
- He was an extremely **conscientious** worker.
- Your ability to compose **rigorous** and **systematic** evaluations is thus crucial to your academic and professional success.
- He seemed to have given up all hope of finding work again, seemed lazy, **sloppy**, and **careless**.
- He needed to sort out the **chaotic** mess of papers on his desk.

3 **Now listen again, stop the recording as necessary and complete the gaps in the sentences.**

1 My day really is quite ....
2 Your day will be .... by a manager coming up to you.
3 We've ...., so I'm devising a programme that I can roll out next week.
4 So they're the things I'd like ....
5 They're all at .... – one of them might be at, you know, advertising stage.
6 So it's, you know, it's so .... to get it right.

John uses quite a lot of business jargon. Here are some interesting and useful terms that he used:

to be thrown by	to be up to
to make sure	to let things slip
to get it right	to work out

Check the meaning of these words in the mini-dictionary and then play the recording again to check your understanding.

B **Anna is a television producer from the south of England. What would you expect her daily routine to involve?**

1 **Play the recording through once. Are these statements true or false?**

	True	False
1 Anna spends most of her time in an office environment.		
2 She is always in a leading role at work.		
3 She rarely spends time working out of the office.		
4 She enjoys her work very much.		

Clear usage: clarifying a word or phrase

Note how Anna says:

'... where I am using a film camera, directing *what we call* contributors. A contributor could be a presenter, it could be a person ...'

She is aware that her audience may not be aware of the meaning of the word *contributors* in the TV industry and therefore clarifies the word.

Here are some more examples of language used for clarifying and asking for clarification:

A performance review – **that's what we call** *an assessment, an analysis of how well somebody is doing their job.*

What I mean by *'tracking on time'* **is** *that everything is happening according to the agreed schedule.*

I mentioned our PPR system: **PPR stands for** *Performance and Practice Review.*

Could you say more about *what the researcher does?*

Sorry, I didn't understand / don't understand *the word 'meticulous'.*

2 Now listen again. Notice how Anna drops the final 't' in some words and pronounces it strongly in others. Complete the gaps in the following phrases, all of which are words ending in 't'.

1 I spend .... of time speaking to people on the phone.
2 My main role is to provide .... for a television programme.
3 I .... a director.
4 Often I can .... on location and work on shoots.
5 A contributor could be a presenter, ... could be a person that ...

COBUILD CHECK: attitudes to work

- It was a **wide-ranging** job that broadened my perspective of the corporation.
- When clients build up a relationship with me, it makes my job very **rewarding**.
- She had expected the job to be **fun, exciting**, and creative.
- Peter is tired of his **tedious, monotonous** job.
- Some workers may prefer **repetitive** jobs as they can give one a sense of security.

3 Match the adjectives on the left, which describe people's attitudes to their work, with those with similar meanings on the right. The vocabulary can be found in this unit or in the mini-dictionary on page 84.

1 diverse   a tedious
2 boring   b talented
3 exciting   c trustworthy
4 skilful   d wide-ranging
5 reliable   e stimulating

C In the next recording, Mark, who is from Melbourne, Australia, describes his job as a duty manager in a large hotel. Before you listen, what do you think his job might involve? Read the questions below for clues.

1 Read the questions first. Then play the recording once and answer the questions.

1 In which part of the hotel does Mark spend his time?
2 What are his busy times?
3 What kinds of complaints does he receive and deal with?
4 How would he try to put things right for his guests if they have had a bad experience in the hotel?

2 Now listen again. Complete the phrases for detailed comprehension. Are there any aspects of his pronunciation which cause you listening problems, or do you find Mark easy to understand?

1 And then in the afternoon to evening, where .... are coming in.
2 I look after a lot of the ...., feedback, and also complaints.
3 So anything to do with a guest coming to the hotel that's .... or had a dissatisfied stay (standard English = ... or being dissatisfied with their stay).
4 I would then try to .... that or, you know, follow that up.
5 ... and see if I can somehow .... their stay for the next couple of days.
6 Looking after them in any sort of general way, sort of .... their expectations.

Clear usage: 'consist of'

Note how Mark says that his job *consists of* looking after the guests at his hotel.

Other useful phrases used for describing job responsibilities:

*The job **includes** dealing with complaints.*

*It **comprises** managing a small team.*

*It **entails** dealing with customers who are arriving and departing.*

3 Match the verbs taken from the recording (on the left) with phrases that have similar meanings (on the right). Check the words as they are used in the recording.

1 to consist of
2 to rectify
3 to enhance
4 to exceed
5 to chase up

a to make better
b to go beyond / further
c to put right
d to check what has happened
e to comprise

FURTHER LISTENING

Listen to the recordings again and read through the transcripts. For further recordings of all of the speakers in this unit, go to the website, **www.collinselt.com/listening**.

15 LEARNING AND USING ENGLISH

BEFORE YOU LISTEN

In this unit you will hear three speakers talking about their experiences of learning and using English. Consider your own experience of learning English.

- What were the difficulties?
- What were your main motivating factors?
- Have you made special efforts to work on your accent to ensure that you are understood more easily?

A The first recording features Eva who is originally from Salzburg in Austria. She spent a year studying in the UK and needs to use English on a daily basis.

1 Play the recording through once. Are these statements true or false? Does anything surprise you about what she says?

	True	False
1 Eva adapted quickly to using English when she came to live in the UK.		
2 She is happy that she continues to speak English with an accent.		
3 Eva still has difficulty understanding many English accents.		
4 By the end of her year, she preferred writing in English to writing in German.		

Leicester (pronounced *less-tuh*) is a culturally diverse city with a population of around 300,000; it is situated in the centre of England.

'The Erasmus scheme' is an exchange programme in which university students from European countries are given the opportunity to study in a different country within the European Union.

COBUILD CHECK: learning a language

- Learning and teaching are **enriching** experiences for both the student and the teacher.
- It was a very **exhausting** experience just to have a conversation.
- The language learning process is innately **rewarding**.
- The proposals are intended to encourage learners to **persevere** with languages.

2 Now listen again, stop the recording as necessary and complete the gaps in the sentences.

1 When I was .... my Erasmus year in Leicester …

2 I .... with lots of different international people.

3 The words just come out of your mouth and you don't really .... about it anymore.

4 I got to know lots of different foreign ....

5 So my ability to, kind of, like .... accents and also to understand foreign accents really improved.

6 I always found that English is .... as a language.

7 German has lots of very long and, you know, ..., whereas English is straight to the point.

8 I preferred writing in .... language, I suppose.

As you listen to the recording, notice Eva's frequent use of 'filler' language such as 'kind of', 'kind of like', 'you know', 'I guess', and 'I suppose'. Filler language is useful because it gives the speaker time to think and the listener more time to follow. That said, such language should not be overused.

3 Read the following phrases, each taken from the recording. In which order do they appear in the audio?

1 I always appreciated English for that.

2 Your language reveals that …

3 English is much more precise.

4 You adapt very, very quickly.

5 We had to communicate in English.

6 It's exhausting, in a way.   ....

After you listen

• Eva says that learning a language is an 'enriching' experience. Do you agree?

• She also talks about how she 'develops a personality' in the language she is using. Do you think that this is the case for you? Can you imagine what she means by this?

B You are now going to listen to Louisa, who is from Germany. She has lived and worked in Canada and the UK.

1 In this recording, Louisa talks about her experience of learning English. Play the recording through once and answer these general comprehension questions.

1 When did Louisa start learning English?

2 How does she feel about speaking English?

3 What is her opinion of the general standard of English pronunciation from German speakers of English?

4 Why does she think she 'does not have an accent' when speaking English?

> Louisa describes German as being 'a very monotone language' and English as having more 'ups and downs'. How would you describe the *intonation* of your language? Do you agree with Louisa's generalizations concerning English? If you know German, do you agree with her opinions about German?

2 **Now listen again to check your detailed comprehension. Complete the phrases.**

1 I think I can .... more in English than in German.

2 We have a really ...., especially in English.

3 They had (those) that .... which is really funny.

4 And well, I'm .... about English.

5 I don't really have .... German accent.

3 **Listen again and note down some of the phrases Louisa uses which demonstrate her great enthusiasm for learning and using English. Listen out for phrases like the following:** *enjoy, feel comfortable, love, passionate, glad*

Example: .....*I always enjoyed it*...

....

....

....

....

C **Kwadwo is from Ghana and has lived in the UK for nine years. In this recording, he talks about his attitude to learning a 'British accent' as part of assimilating into society.**

1 **Play the recording through once. Which one of these statements best describes Kwadwo's attitude to using English?**

1 He is keen to learn to speak with an English accent.

2 He would like to use slang terms such as 'innit'.

3 He believes that people understand him when he speaks English.

4 He would not try to change his accent even if people did not understand him.

> Note that Kwadwo says 'hear' when the 'standard' English verb would be 'understand' or 'listen' (depending on the context). This is a typical Ghanaian English usage of the word 'hear'.
>
> Can you spot any other things Kwadwo says that you would not think of as standard English? Did you understand what he meant anyway?

2 Now listen again as you read the following words and phrases. Focus on any words and phrases that you find difficult to understand and underline them. As you play the recording again, familiarize yourself with the way Kwadwo pronounces these.

You've never picked the accent.

I don't want to be in the shoes of somebody whom I don't know.

The youth in my country would love to behave like Americans, with their jeans coming off.

I don't see it attractive.

Whenever I speak to him and I don't say anything of that sort ...

So I guess that's the main reason why he said my accent hasn't changed.

If they don't hear me when I speak, that is different.

Since they hear whatever I wanna say to them, I don't think I have a problem.

Kwadwo says that he does not want to use slang such as 'innit'. This expression is used by some UK speakers at the end of sentences as a question tag instead of the standard forms: isn't it?, aren't they?, isn't he / she?, etc. It is also increasingly used as a phrase to end any sentence!

'Stuff' is an informal word for 'things'. Kwadwo also says 'for sign languages and stuff'. 'Stuff' is sometimes used when the speaker does not know how to end a sentence. It is also used as an informal / slang term for 'things' and 'related topics'.

Some examples:

There was a lot of talk at the conference about globalization and stuff.

I've got a lot of homework and stuff to do this afternoon.

What a lot of stuff you've got in your flat!

You need to get rid of some stuff.

What really interests me is the stuff about the president's wife.

3 Listen to the recording once more and identify phrases used by Kwadwo that are the equivalent to the following 'standard' English statements.

1 You've never picked up the accent.

2 I don't want to try to be like someone who is not like me.

3 Speaking with their hands – gestures and things like that.

4 I don't see that as being attractive.

5 If they don't understand me when I speak, that is different.

FURTHER LISTENING

Listen to the recordings again and read through the transcripts. For further recordings of the speakers in this unit, go to the website, **www.collinselt.com/listening**.

16 HOBBIES AND INTERESTS

BEFORE YOU LISTEN

The speakers in this unit discuss a range of hobbies and interests.

- What are your hobbies and special interests?
- Are any of these unusual or particular to your country / region?
- How would you describe them in a way that makes them sound interesting to a listener?

A In this recording, Hannah, who was born in Australia but has lived in the UK for much of her life, talks about her passions for cooking and blogging.

1 Read the general comprehension questions below. Then play the recording through once and answer each question.

1 Who passed on a love of cooking to Hannah?
2 Which countries have influenced the food she cooks?
3 Why did she start writing a food blog?
4 How does writing a blog make her feel?
5 When does she find her blog particularly useful?

Clear usage: using the continuous form of the verb

Hannah is an enthusiastic speaker. Note how she uses the continuous form of the verb to emphasize feelings and events combined with the colloquial expressions *to go on about* and *to get someone doing / asking*. Compare:

'I'm always going on about food' = *I talk a lot about food.*

'I was always getting people asking me' = *People often used to ask me about.*

---

2 Listen again and note down the dishes that Hannah likes to cook. Do you like to cook similar food? What type of food do you like to cook / eat?

....

....

....

....

Useful vocabulary and phrases: cooking

Can I have the recipe?

How did you make that?

Is there anything you don't eat?

I'm allergic to seafood.

Have you ever tried frogs' legs?

What are the main ingredients?

I have a wheat allergy.

I'm a vegetarian.

COBUILD CHECK: social networking

- Now she has a website where she writes a daily **blog**.
- The downturn will also accelerate the use of social media, such as blogs and **social-networking sites**.
- Most politicians **tweet** to promote themselves.
- It is now the top **trending topic**.

3 Now listen again, stop the recording as necessary and complete the gaps in the sentences.

1 We really love to ………………… and have big meals.

2 So whether it's a big …………..………..……………… or whether it's a tortilla from Spain …

3 I get the best recipes that I cook and ………………… there.

4 We'd be sharing ………………… .

5 Why not put it there, so that they can ………………… it themselves?

4 Complete the phrases on the left by matching them with phrases from the right.

1 It's a real ………   a meatballs

2 I put something on ………   b family passion

3 It's surprisingly ………   c my own voice

4 I like the sound of ………   d my blog

5 They can download ………   e relaxing

6 It's pasta filled with ………   f the recipe

B In this recording, Alex talks about keeping pets. Alex lives in the countryside, just outside London. Try to predict the types of animals he keeps.

1 Play the recording through once. Are these statements true or false?

	True	False
1 Alex's family keeps chickens at the bottom of the garden.		
2 His children enjoy collecting the eggs.		
3 His neighbours don't seem to enjoy being woken up by the cockerel.		
4 He has definitely decided to get rid of the cockerel.		
5 His parents do not keep chickens.		

Alex says that his neighbours had 'slightly gritted teeth' when they said they were happy for him to keep a cockerel (a male chicken). If you do something through 'gritted teeth' it means that you accept something against your will – but other people can see how you really feel.

Note also the understatement implied by the word 'slightly'. Can you imagine the difference in effect if Alex had not included the word 'slightly'?

2 **Now listen again. Complete these phrases, which express Alex's uncertainty about keeping the cockerel.**

1 Summer is probably ……………..……................. to get a cockerel.

2 The cockerel's …………..……….................. everybody that he's up.

3 We ……....…….……..................... ask the neighbours if it was going to be a problem.

4 I think they had slightly ……....…….…….................. when they said that.

5 He may …….....………....…................... back.

Clear usage: using 'did' to emphasize past actions and thoughts

Note how Alex uses *did* ('We did ask the neighbours') for emphasis. Contrast the emphatic use of *did* with the simple past in these examples:

I spoke to them. / I did speak to them.

I rang him. / I did ring him.

I knew the answer. / I did know the answer.

I believed her. / I did believe her.

I understood what she said. / I really did understand what she said.

Can you sense the change in emphasis in each of the above examples? Listen out for other speakers doing the same thing in the other recordings on the CD.

C **In this recording, you will hear James talking about his passion for music. Is this passion something that you share? How would you describe your interest in music?**

39

1 **Read the questions below. Then, listen to the recording and answer each question.**

1 How often does James's band practise?

2 Why do they find it difficult to practise more often?

3 What does James rarely have time for?

4 What would he like to do more often?

When James says that music takes up 'a fair bit of my time', he means that it takes up a lot of his time. Expressions such as 'a fair bit' are typical of native UK English understatement.

Clear usage: showing enthusiasm

Note the phrases that James uses to demonstrate his enthusiasm for his hobby:

'I'm constantly listening to music and playing it whenever I have spare time.'

'I would say I'm very interested in going to see other people's live music.'

'I would love to go to more.'

'It's something that I would like to do more of.'

2 **Now listen again, stop the recording as necessary to check your detailed comprehension, and complete the gaps in the sentences.**

1 The band tries to practise ...., if we can.

2 We do .... as much as possible.

3 I'm .... listening to music and playing it whenever I have spare time.

4 I don't go to enough ....

5 There are .... very, very good open-mic nights.

6 It's just a .... knowing where they are.

COBUILD CHECK: music

- He is the singer in a successful local **rock band**.
- They sat on the sofa, **listening to music** on the radio.
- The group **played a gig** at the city's Supper Club last night.
- The band **played to** a rapturous crowd.
- He'd do little shows here and there, sometimes **open-mic nights** at bars in the city.
- He asked me if I wanted to go to a **music festival** with him.

3 **James uses a number of the following expressions of time. Listen to the recording and underline the ones he uses. Write down what he does.**

Example: Once a week – the band tries to practise once a week

twice a week	every month
once a month	I try to find time
five times a month	whenever I have spare time
every day	I very rarely have the time
every week	a fair bit of my time

FURTHER LISTENING

Listen to the recordings again and read through the transcripts. For further recordings including a recording of a German speaker of English who enjoys blogging about fashion in English, go to **www.collinselt.com/listening**.

17 SOCIALIZING

BEFORE YOU LISTEN

In this unit, you will hear two very different accounts of socializing – by day and by night.

- Do you prefer to socialize mainly with family and existing friends?
- Do you prefer socializing at home or when going out?
- How do you usually meet new people? Would you strike up a conversation in a café, for example?
- Would you join a club or a society to meet new people?
- Do you use the Internet to make new friends and keep up with old ones?
- As you listen to the speakers in this unit, consider who you have most in common with.

A What do you think Lisa, a young professional, focuses on when she describes going out for an evening in her home town of Newcastle in the north east of England? You may be surprised.

1 Play the recording through once. Are these statements true or false? **True** **False**

1 It's expensive to go out for the evening in Newcastle.
2 When you go out for an evening in Newcastle, you have to have a clear plan of where to go.
3 In Newcastle, you have to walk a lot between bars.
4 People in Newcastle always wear coats when they go out on a cold evening.
5 You don't need to wear a coat, because you usually take a taxi home.

COBUILD CHECK: being sociable

- I try to **socialize with** colleagues, but find it hard to break into their circles.
- I probably don't push myself to **get out and meet people** as much as I should.
- A lot of people I know **go out** every weekend, but I don't, because I can't afford to.
- He enjoys **partying** with friends.
- This is the time to be more **outgoing and sociable**.
- Describing himself as shy and **anti-social**, he tried internet dating.
- Once a **gregarious**, outgoing, happy child, she is now withdrawn.

Lisa is from Newcastle, a city of approximately 200,000 people in the north east of England. Go to **www.collinsmaps.com** to find Newcastle on a map. Natives of Newcastle are sometimes referred to as 'Geordies'. Geordies have a very distinctive accent, although Lisa has a very mild form of the local accent.

Lisa talks about 'hen dos' and 'stag parties'. Such nights are typically when groups of women (hens) or groups of men (stags) go out with the bride or groom shortly before a wedding to celebrate the upcoming event and to say goodbye to their single life. A 'do' is slang for a party or gathering.

2 **Now listen again, stop the recording as necessary, and complete the gaps in the sentences.**

1 It's quite a …….................. place to go for a night out.
2 … even though it's a …….................. compared to London.
3 There's a …….................., I think around Europe, that …
4 When I go out in London, …….................. take a coat.
5 All the places you want to go …….................. in a small area.
6 So in a way, it kind of …….................. .

Clear usage: 'get'

Get is often used in spoken English instead of words and expressions such as *arrive*, *be* (particularly in passive sentences), and *take*. Note the phrases that Lisa uses:

'get to town' = arrive in town
'get picked up' = be picked up
'get a taxi' = take a taxi

Some other examples:

I got to the office at 9 am. = I arrived at the office at 9 am.
I get invited to a lot of parties. = I am asked to a lot of parties.
I got the bus this morning. = I took the bus this morning.
I often get told that I sound American. = I am often told that I sound American.
I usually get the train to work. = I usually take the train to work.

3 **Complete the sentences by matching the start of the phrase (on the left) with the correct ending (on the right).**

1 You don't really need a coat because you're   a concentrated in a small area.
2 You don't need to plan   b not outside so much.
3 People from Newcastle don't   c where you're going out.
4 All the places you want to go are   d bars to choose from.
5 You don't have to walk   e wear coats when they go out.
6 There are lots and lots of   f a great deal.

B In this recording, Maria, who is originally from Ireland but is currently living in a small village in England, describes a very 'English' social event, the village fête. What would you expect to find at such an event? As you listen, reflect on how this event contrasts with local events and festivals where you live.

1 Read the questions below, and then play the recording through once. Answer the questions to test your general comprehension. There is some vocabulary in the box below that will help you.

1 Where in the village does the fête take place?

2 Where does the money that is raised at the fête go?

3 Which event does she describe as being 'a winner'?

4 What could you buy from the stalls that were set up?

5 What was the weather like on the day of the fête?

Maria refers to the 'handsomest hound' competition in the dog show. A 'hound' is a dog, so this is a special name for a competition to the find the most attractive / most handsome dog. The aim of such competitions is normally to raise money for charity while having some fun. Prizes may be given to the person who has grown the largest vegetable in a village, who has correctly guessed the weight of a cake, or who has thrown a wellington boot the furthest.

Useful vocabulary and phrases: the village fête

Many of these terms may be unfamiliar to you so check them in the mini-dictionary or in your bilingual dictionary.

fête	charity	proceeds	coconut shy	scarecrow
donkey rides	raffle	stalls	cricket green	relay races

Clear usage: some active and passive past tenses

Check the recording and transcript for the way Maria uses these tenses:

1 Simple past passive: *We **were all asked** to donate something for the raffle.*

The active equivalent: *They asked us to donate something for the raffle.*

Other passive examples: *We **were sent** personal invitations to the show.*

*The children **were given** prizes.*

2 Past perfect: *The kids **had made** scarecrows.*

The passive equivalent: *The scarecrows had been made by the children.*

Other active examples: *The fête was a great success because everyone **had worked** so hard setting everything up.*

*My neighbour **had won** the raffle last year and won it again this year.*

2 Now listen again and complete the phrases.

1 It happens .... a year in Shamley Green where I live.
2 We've got one shop and .... and a cricket green.
3 We were .... as neighbours in the village to donate something.
4 There was a .... where the kids the week before in the primary school had made scarecrows.
5 Also relay races with the kids and .... for the children.
6 Just various .... and a few stalls where you can buy ...

3 Rewrite these active sentences in the passive, as in the example.

Example: The village committee made all the arrangements.

All of the arrangements were made by the village committee.
....

1 They had already discussed the plans at their weekly meeting.
The plans ....
2 They gave all of the proceeds to charity.
All of the proceeds ....
3 They presented the organizer with a large box of chocolates.
The organizer ....
4 They awarded Fido the title of 'handsomest hound'.
Fido ....
5 The children had made the scarecrows in their primary schools.
The scarecrows ....

COBUILD CHECK: charity and charities

- Thousands of items of clothing were **donated by** the public to help the victims of the flooding.
- If you would like to **make a donation**, please fill in and return the coupon below.
- All profits will **go to charity**.
- The **proceeds** from the event go to charity.
- Don't forget, all this money goes to **good causes**.
- Several **charities** for the homeless are considering merging.

FURTHER LISTENING

Listen to the recordings again and read through the transcripts. For further recordings of Lisa and Maria, go to the website **www.collinselt.com/listening**.

18 KEEPING FIT AND HEALTHY

BEFORE YOU LISTEN

This unit is all about diet, lifestyle, and fitness. Compare your thoughts on this subject with those expressed in the recordings.

- How do you keep fit and healthy?
- Do you go to a gym / health club?
- Do you prefer to walk or cycle than drive or take the bus?
- Do you keep healthy by sticking to a good diet?

A In the first recording, a gym receptionist from London describes gym facilities to Holly, a potential member.

1 Read the questions below. Then play the recording through once and answer the questions to check your general understanding.

1 What are the two rooms in the gym used for?
2 Why might the swimming pool be busy in the middle of the day?
3 What is the best time to come to the pool for a quiet swim?
4 What kind of ID (identification) do you need to show if you wish to join the gym?

2 Note the specific language used to talk about the gym and swimming pool facilities. Check that you understand the meaning of the following terms by referring to the mini-dictionary. Then listen to the recording again and complete the sentences.

treadmills	mirrors	exercises	weightlifting	aero-biking	lanes

1 We have one room for the ....
2 ... and the other side is for the ....
3 They have a bike section for the .... as well.
4 And also they have ....
5 Do they have quite a lot of .... there?
6 In the .... swims, do you have different speeds?

Clear usage: agreement and reinforcement

Note the language used by Holly in response to the information given by the receptionist. She shows that she is fully engaged with what the receptionist is telling her. Listen again and focus on how she uses this language:

'Right.'

'Okay, my favourite ...'

'Alright, that's really good.
And what about ...?'

'Right, okay.'

'Cool.' (in informal language
    cool = *very good*)

'Good, that's useful.'

'Okay, perfect. That sounds great.'

'Great, thank you very much.'

3 Listen again as you read the following words and phrases. Focus on the words that you find difficult to understand and underline them. Familiarize yourself with the way the receptionist pronounces certain sounds.

For example: 'th' as 'd'
                the final 'l' in some words as 'w'
                'ng' as 'n'

They have (a) bike section for the aero-biking, as well. And also they have mirrors.

The pool is twenty-five metres ...

When we have swimming lessons.

Till we close, it's quite calm then.

That's like, something like your passport and a bill with your address.

Okay then, thank you.

B In this recording, Holly meets a fitness instructor and discusses the need for a healthy diet. What kinds of questions might you expect Holly to ask him? What advice would you expect him to give?

1 Play the recording through once. Are these statements true or false? Note that the fitness instructor also has a London accent. Compare it with that of the receptionist you listened to in the first recording.

	True	False

1   He advises her to eat nuts and raisins before going to the gym.

2   The instructor believes that when you eat and how much you eat are more important than what you eat.

3   He advises her to use the stairs rather than using the lift.

4   He advises her not to sit down while she is working.

5   He thinks that if you exercise regularly, you feel better within yourself and you feel more active.

Note that the instructor says: 'They're gonna feel better within theirself.'
Standard English would be: *They are going to feel better within themselves.*

Clear usage: giving advice

Notice how the instructor varies the way he gives advice. First, he addresses his advice directly to Holly:

'After *you've* finished *your* workout, then *you'd* probably eat something.'
'I wouldn't tell *you* that *you* can't eat this or can't eat, that but obviously watch the amount and the times when *you're* having it.'

Then at other times, the instructor gives advice indirectly:

'I would try and get over to *them*.'
'*They're* just generally getting more active.'

Sometimes he wants to personalize the advice and at other times, he talks objectively about how he helps all of his clients.

2 **Now listen again and focus on the specific requests for advice and on the advice given. Complete the phrases.**

1 I'm never really sure if ...., or what I should be eating before I do exercise.

2 After you've ...., then you'd probably eat something a bit more balanced.

3 So I .... you that you can't eat this or can't eat that.

4 But obviously watch .... when you're having it.

5 Forget about the ...., take the ....

6 Make sure you've got a good ...., no .... and things like that ...

COBUILD CHECK: fitness and exercise

- Regular **exercise** helps to combat unwanted stress and is a good way of relaxing.
- After a strenuous **workout**, you get a great feeling of well-being.
- His advice to anyone starting a **fitness** regime is to take it easy.
- I knew I wouldn't get to sleep if I didn't work off some of my excess **energy**.
- Correct breathing, **good posture**, and deep relaxation encourage the body to function more efficiently.

3 **Match the verbs taken from the recording (on the left) with words that have similar meanings (on the right).**

1	posture	a	fitness training
2	nutrition	b	quantity
3	exercise	c	diet
4	amount	d	vitality
5	energy	e	way of standing / sitting

C The final speaker in this unit is Tare from New Zealand. He regularly works out at a gym and in this recording he talks about why he wants to keep fit.

1 Read the questions first. Then play the recording through once and answer each question.

1 What is the main reason Tare gives for going to the gym regularly?

2 What does he want to do with his family when he is forty?

3 Does he enjoy going to the gym?

4 How does he feel after a session in the gym?

Tare says he does not want to have a 'pot belly' = a large stomach

---

Useful vocabulary and phrases: weight and diet

I am trying to lose weight.

I need to put on some weight.

I am a little overweight / underweight.

I need to avoid fatty foods.

I need to cut down on the amount of salt I eat.

I am trying to stick to a healthy diet.

I try to exercise three times a week.

I don't believe in dieting – I think you're best to allow yourself everything in moderation.

---

2 Now listen again to check your detailed understanding. Complete the phrases.

1 I look around and a lot of men (sort of) get to .... old.

2 They've really .... and, you know, I don't want to be in that position.

3 Maybe somewhat you could put it down to ...., I don't know.

4 I don't want to be forty years old, when I eventually ...., and not be able to ...

5 Everyday living can be ....

6 I don't think anybody actually enjoys .... Well, I know ...

7 Once you're there, you just kind of go into .... mode.

8 It just helps me (sort of) .... and gives me energy to just .... with everyday life.

FURTHER LISTENING

Listen to the recordings again and read through the transcripts. For more recordings from the gym and of Tare describing details of his workouts, go to **www.collinselt.com/listening**.

19 EATING IN AND EATING OUT

BEFORE YOU LISTEN

The recordings in this unit feature speakers talking about eating out in restaurants and eating at home. Compare your experiences with those of the speakers.

- Do you prefer home cooking or restaurant food?
- Do you have a favourite restaurant?
- Have you had any unusual eating experiences?
- Are you quite adventurous with food? Do you like trying new things?

A In this recording, Catherine, who is from London, talks about her experience of eating out in Seoul in South Korea.

1 Read the questions below. Then play the recording through once and answer the questions.

1 Why did Catherine decide to go into a Korean barbecue restaurant?
2 Why was she nervous about going inside?
3 How did she know how to eat the food in the restaurant?
4 Did she enjoy the food and the restaurant?

In this recording, Catherine explained how Korean barbecue works. Did you understand her explanation? Have you ever had Korean barbecue?

Check that you understand the specific words in the recording relating to the barbecue by looking them up in the mini-dictionary or in your own bilingual dictionary. Look up these words that Catherine used: 'pit', 'coals', and 'extractor'.

Useful vocabulary and phrases: food preparation

barbecued [UK] / grilled [US]	steamed
boiled	fermented
fried	pickled
grilled [UK] / broiled [US]	wrapped
stuffed	marinated

2 **Now listen again. Stop the recording as necessary and complete the gaps in the sentences.**

1 Actually that place smelled ...., I'm gonna try and find it again.

2 So you put the meat .... there into the lettuce leaf, you wrap it up ...

3 You can choose some *kimchi* which you .... in Korea.

4 You can have a different kind of .... every time.

5 But I had .... I was there on my own ...

6 The waitress and I understood .... just enough to order and pay.

Clear usage: expressing emotions

Catherine gives the impression of being surprised at how much she enjoyed her experience of eating out, alone, in a restaurant where she did not know the local language. Note the phrases she uses:

'I was *a little bit nervous* of going in.'

'I *wasn't quite sure* what I was going to find.'

'... sort of pickled cabbage, which is delicious, *actually*.' (Using *actually* shows that she was surprised by her reaction to it.)

'I was *a bit self-conscious*.'

'I *was very pleased I had been brave enough* to go in.'

---

3 **Catherine says, 'You put the barbecued meat – which has been barbecued in front of you by the waitress – into the lettuce leaf.' She does not barbecue the meat herself – it is 'done for her'. Rewrite the following active sentences into the passive (present or present perfect).**

Example: They have changed the menu.

The menu has been changed.

1 They have eaten all of the kimchi.

All of the kimchi ....

2 They usually barbecue the meat for you.

The meat ....

3 You wrap the meat in the lettuce leaf.

The meat ....

4 Do you often dress salads with oil here?

Is the salad ....?

5 Have you cooked the main course yet?

Has the main course ....?

6 Do you ever eat octopus while it is still alive?

Is octopus ....?

B Maria is from a small village in Ireland. In this recording, she talks about what types of meals she and her husband Simon like to cook, and about what types of restaurants they like to go to.

1 Read the general comprehension questions below. Then play the recording through once and answer the questions.

1 Why does Maria not have to prepare dinner on weekday evenings?
2 What kind of food does she like to cook at the weekends?
3 Do Maria and her husband eat out much?
4 Is Maria a good cook?

Clear usage: 'used to'

Maria makes it clear that she no longer lives next door to the 'old neighbours' (old as in *previous*, not necessarily old in terms of age) who she recently had a meal with by using the *used to* form of the verb. Note the contrast with the simple past used to describe simple, completed actions (*met* and *went*).

'Last weekend *we met* with our old neighbours that *we used to live* beside, and *we went* to an Italian restaurant across the road from them.'

Other examples:

We often used to go out for meals together.

We used to have a lot of dinner parties, but we're too busy now.

Did you use to go to the Mexican restaurant in the centre of town?

There used to be a lovely bistro on the corner over there, but it closed down last year.

---

2 Now listen again for detailed comprehension of what may be some unfamiliar vocabulary and complete the gaps. Can you work out the meanings of any unfamiliar words and phrases from the context of the recording? When you have finished the exercise, check the mini-dictionary.

1 I try and get him to .... (from) the norm, from time to time.
2 I'd do the more .... things that you'd get back home.
3 You know, sweet and .... salads and things like that.
4 I don't .... to be the world's greatest chef.
5 We .... to go out a lot. There's just the two of us so ...
6 I like to .... So we ...

Maria says that her husband Simon's cooking is 'regimented', in other words not very imaginative! By using this term, she is suggesting that Simon's cooking is possibly too controlled and organized. 'Regimented' derives from the army word 'regiment'.

Maria also mentioned the names of lots of typical Irish dishes. Look at the transcript if you are unfamiliar with any of the names she mentions.

COBUILD CHECK: meet

- We could **meet** for a drink after work.
- We tend to **meet up** for lunch once a week.
- He's asked to **meet with** you later today.
- I occasionally **meet up with** him for coffee or a drink.
- I'd never **met** him before that night but we immediately felt like old friends.

After you listen

- Would you enjoy eating the home-cooked food described by Maria?
- How does it differ from the food that you normally eat at home?
- Where you live, do men or women do most of the cooking or is the preparation of food shared equally?

C You will now hear a very short recording in which Tare, a New Zealander, talks about one of his favourite restaurants in Sydney, Australia. How would you describe your favourite restaurant?

1 Play the recording through once. Which one of the three statements best represents his feelings about the restaurant?

1 He mainly went there for the great food.

2 He mainly went for the great company.

3 For him, the service was the best thing about the restaurant.

2 Now listen again and focus on all the positive language used to describe the restaurant. In which order do these positive phrases appear in the dialogue?

1 But **more than anything**, I liked the service there.

2 **We'd recommend it** to other people.

3 The guy that owned the restaurant was **really friendly**.

4 It was **just a nice family-run**, (just a) small place.

5 The food **was great**.

6 There was a **nice little Thai restaurant** …   ……. ……. ……. ……. ……. …….

FURTHER LISTENING

Listen to the recordings again and read through the transcripts. For further recordings including more from Catherine, stories of favourite foods and restaurants, go to **www.collinselt.com/listening**.

20 SPORT

Before you listen to the recordings in this unit, think about how you would describe your sporting interests. Then compare them with those described by the speakers.

- What are your favourite sports?
- Do you prefer to play sport or would you rather watch?
- Are there any sports you hate? Why?

A In this recording, James talks about his interest in 'touch rugby'. What do you think this sport is? How do you think it might be played?

1 Listen to the recording and then decide whether the statements are true or false.

	True	False
1 The key point of touch rugby is to put people on the ground.		
2 It is a very fast game.		
3 You touch your opponent with one hand and then the game stops.		
4 Men and women can play in the same team.		

James focuses on 'touch rugby', but he also refers to 'rugby union', a very popular sport with fifteen players on each side. 'Rugby league' is another version of rugby and there are some differences in the rules. Rugby league has thirteen players on each side.

2 This recording probably includes a number of words that are unfamiliar to you. Listen to the recording again and pause after these phrases. Can you work out what they mean from the context? Check in the mini-dictionary or in your own bilingual dictionary.

The <u>full contact</u> side of the game.

<u>Tackling</u> and putting people on the ground.

Stepping on them in the <u>mud</u>.

If there's been no <u>score</u>, then the ball will go over to the other [side].

Without too much <u>damage</u> to <u>reputation</u> or to body.

Useful vocabulary and phrases: playing sport

I have been playing rugby since I was five.
I play for a local team.
I play competitively.
I just play for fun with friends in the park.
I had to give up playing squash when I hurt my wrist.
I've decided to take up tennis.
Do you play any / much sport?
I'm a huge football fan.
I much prefer watching sport to playing it.

COBUILD CHECK: sport

- Stock-car racing is one of America's largest **spectator sports**.
- Hockey is a **contact sport** and injuries will occur.
- Not only is badminton the fastest **racket sport**, but it is also the most popular.
- The new subscription **sports channel** is to be launched in August.
- As a child, I was always very **sporty**.
- It is a paradise for people who love **winter sports**.

3 Match the words from the recording (on the left) with those with a similar meaning (on the right).

1	form	a	injury
2	simpler	b	type
3	the other side	c	easier
4	damage	d	the opposite team

After you listen

- Having listened to James, do you feel that you have learned something about touch rugby?
- Is there more you would have liked to ask him?
- Find someone who does not know the rules of touch rugby and explain the rules to him or her.
- How would you explain your favourite sport to someone who has not seen it or played it and does not know the rules?

B In this next track, you will hear Iwona from Poland talking about her passion for skiing.

1 Play the recording through once. Which one of the following statements best represents Iwona's attitude towards skiing?

1 You will enjoy it most if you can go skiing with the whole family.
2 You need to have the best skiing equipment you can buy.
3 You must have proper skiing instruction.
4 The best skiing is to be found in the Czech Republic.

In common with other Polish speakers of English, Iwona does not always follow standard rules in her use of auxiliary verbs, articles, and plural forms.

Note these phrases that Iwona uses:

'I just want to do skiing every day' = *I just want to go skiing every day*

'a very long, old-fashioned skis' = *very long, old-fashioned skis*

'they didn't have a proper stoppers, you know, like a professional one' = *they didn't have proper stoppers – you know, like professional ones do*

'to Czech Republic' = *to the Czech Republic*

2 **How easy do you find it to understand Iwona's English? Do you have problems understanding her pronunciation or her grammar? Listen again to how she pronounces the following phrases and underline any words and phrases that you find difficult to understand.**

I just want to do skiing every day.

My parents never skied before, so I didn't have this kind of culture in my family.

I actually took from my gran – sorry from my godmother – a very long, old-fashioned skis.

I almost killed my friends at the same time.

My mum managed to actually send me every winter to (the) Czech Republic.

Skiing is very similar to playing golf actually.

COBUILD CHECK: sports equipment

- **Cross-country skis** are finer than normal skis.
- There are, in a normal set of **golf clubs**, about ten irons and three woods.
- There were various items of **sports gear** on the back seat of the car.
- Kids ran onto the field carrying **baseball bats**.
- **Scuba gear** can be rented from dive shops located along White Beach.
- I changed into shorts, a T-shirt, **tennis shoes** and socks.

3 **Now listen again and check your detailed understanding. Complete the phrases.**

1 My mum, I remember sending me off ………………… in [the] Czech Republic.

2 I [had] to shout at my friends like, you know, 'Be careful, because ………………… down!'

3 My mum ………………… to actually send me every winter.

4 You just need to go to a proper ………………… and you need to have a proper instructor.

5 You could learn ………………… for ten years and you will be at the same level.

6 You ………………… progress.

C **In this recording, Vincent, a French Canadian from Quebec, talks about his particular passion: ice hockey. He claims that ice hockey is extremely important in Canada. Which sports create the same level of enthusiasm in your country?**

1 Play the recording through once. Answer these questions to check your general understanding.

1 How often would Vincent go to watch ice hockey if he could?

2 How do people feel if they manage to get hold of a ticket to a hockey game?

3 How does he rate hockey compared with football?

Hockey

The equipment you need: stick, puck (a small disc of hard rubber – to act as the 'ball'), skates, a helmet, a shirt, socks, and lots of protective pads!

Where you play: on an ice rink

Where you watch: in a stadium

Where it is popular: Most popular in Canada, but also played and followed in other northern-hemisphere countries including America, Russia, Sweden, and the Czech Republic.

2 Now listen again and check your detailed listening. Complete the phrases. Focus also on aspects of Vincent's accent which cause you any comprehension difficulties.

1 Well it's also the …...................... in Canada.

2 We follow every match …...................... .

3 It's really easy for us to play hockey, just need a stick, some …...................... , and a puck.

4 I don't know why it's …...................... in the rest of the world.

5 It's …...................... than football, way more …...................... .

6 When someone …...................... , he doesn't cry.

COBUILD CHECK: sports venues

• The centre will have two international-size **hockey rinks**, as well as fitness facilities.

• When it opens, it will be Europe's largest **football stadium**.

• I think it's the best **baseball park** I've ever seen.

• It boasted a championship **golf course**, twelve **tennis courts**, four **squash courts**, three **swimming pools**, and a **gymnasium**.

• If you go into a **boxing ring**, you must take what comes.

FURTHER LISTENING

Listen to the recordings again and read through the transcripts. For other sports-related recordings and further recordings of these speakers go to **www.collinselt.com/listening**.

MINI-DICTIONARY

 The most difficult words from the recordings are defined here in this mini-dictionary. The definitions are extracts from the *Collins COBUILD Advanced Dictionary, Collins COBUILD Business English Dictionary, Collins COBUILD Phrasal Verbs Dictionary,* and *Collins COBUILD Idioms Dictionary.*

Unit 1

proximity N-UNCOUNT **Proximity to** a place or person is nearness to that place or person. • *Part of the attraction is Darwin's proximity to Asia.* • *Families are no longer in close proximity to each other.*

immediate family ADJ N Your **immediate family** are the members of your family who are most closely related to you, for example your parents, children, brothers, and sisters.

conscious ADJ A **conscious** decision or action is made or done deliberately with you giving your full attention to it. • *I don't think we ever made a conscious decision to have a big family.* • *Make a conscious effort to relax your muscles.*

extended family N-COUNT An **extended family** is a family group which includes relatives such as uncles, aunts, and grandparents, as well as parents, children, cousins, and brothers and sisters. • *The pregnant woman has the support of all the women in her extended family.*

gathering N-COUNT A **gathering** is a group of people meeting together for a particular purpose. • *...the twenty-second annual gathering of the South Pacific Forum.*

short for PHRASE If a name or abbreviation is **short for** another name, it is the short version of that name. • *Her friend Kes (short for Kesewa) was in tears.*

matriarch N-COUNT A **matriarch** is powerful, sometimes elderly female member of a family, for example a grandmother.

period ADV Some people say **period** after stating a fact or opinion when they want to emphasize that they are definite about something and do not want to discuss it further. • *I don't want to do it, period.* [AM]

in BRIT, also use **full stop**

divorce VERB If a man and woman **divorce** or if one of them **divorces** the other, their marriage is legally ended. • *My parents divorced when I was very young.*

Unit 2

bulldoze VERB If people **bulldoze** something such as a building, they knock it down using a bulldozer. • *She protested against developers who wanted to bulldoze her home to build a supermarket.*

forward-thinking ADJ If you describe a person or organization as **forward-thinking**, you approve of the fact that they think about the future or have modern ideas. • *Many forward-thinking scientists now support this view.*

diverse ADJ If a group or range of things is **diverse**, it is made up of a wide variety of things. • *...shops selling a diverse range of gifts.*

rely on VERB If you **rely on** someone or something, you need them and depend on them in order to live or work properly. • *They relied heavily on the advice of their professional advisers.*

take the rail PHRASE If you **take the rail**, you travel on a train. Common usage would be **take the train**. • *The president took the train to his home town.*

proper ADJ You can add **proper** after a word to indicate that you are referring to the central and most important part of a place, event, or object and want to distinguish it from other things which are not regarded as being important or central to it. • *A distinction must be made between archaeology proper and science-based archaeology.*

common land N-UNCOUNT **Common land** is land which everyone is allowed to use.

conscious See Unit 1 definition

commute VERB If you **commute**, you travel between your home and your place of work. • *Mike commutes to London every day.*

rural ADJ **Rural** means having features which are typical of areas that are far away from large towns or cities. • *...the old rural way of life.*

Unit 3

terrain N **Terrain** is used to refer to an area of land or a type of land when you are considering its physical features. • *The terrain changed quickly from farming land to desert.*

lush ADJ If you describe vegetation as **lush**, you mean it is growing well and abundantly. • *After the rains, the garden was looking lush.*

eucalyptus A **eucalyptus** is an evergreen tree, originally from Australia, that provides wood, gum, and an oil that is used in medicines.

warfare N-UNCOUNT **Warfare** is the activity of fighting a war. It is sometimes used to refer to any violent struggle or conflict. • *At times, party rivalries have broken out into open warfare.*

indigenous ADJ **Indigenous** people or things belong to the country in which they are found, rather than coming there or being brought there from another country. • *The Maori people are indigenous to New Zealand.*

mindset N-COUNT If you refer to someone's **mindset**, you mean their general attitudes and the way they typically think about things.

Unit 4

tube N **The tube** is the underground railway system in London. [BRIT] • *I took the tube, then the train and came straight here.*

refurbish VERB To **refurbish** a building or room means to clean it and decorate it and make it more attractive or better equipped. • *We have spent money refurbishing the offices.*

view VERB If you **view** something, you look at it for a particular purpose. • *They came back to view the house again.*

property N A **property** is a building and the land belonging to it. • *This vehicle has been parked on private property.*

gated community N-COUNT A **gated community** is an area of houses and sometimes shops that is surrounded by a wall or fence and has an entrance that is guarded.

porter N-COUNT A **porter** is a person whose job is to be in charge of the entrance of a building such as a hotel. [BRIT]

> in AM, also use **doorman**

> In the text, the speaker uses the word **porterage** which is the service of having a porter.

maisonette N-COUNT A **maisonette** is a flat that usually has a separate door to the outside from other flats in the same building. Many maisonettes are on two floors. [BRIT]

furnished ADJ A **furnished** room or house is available to be rented together with the furniture in it.

plumbing N-UNCOUNT The **plumbing** in a building consists of the water and drainage pipes, baths, and toilets in it. • *The electrics and the plumbing were in working order.*

appliance N-COUNT An **appliance** is a device or machine in your home that you use to do a job such as cleaning or cooking. Appliances are often electrical. • *He could also learn to use the vacuum cleaner, the washing machine, and other household appliances.*

Unit 5

integrate VERB If someone **integrates into** a social group, or **is integrated into** it, they behave in such a way that they become part of the group or are accepted into it. • *The way immigrants integrate in Sweden, she feels, is much more advanced.*

enforce VERB To **enforce** something means to force or cause it to be done or to happen.

no offence CONVENTION Some people say 'no offence' to make it clear that they do not want to upset you, although what they are saying may seem rather rude. • *Dad, you need a bath. No offence.*

clique N-COUNT If you describe a group of people as a **clique**, you mean that they spend a lot of time together and seem unfriendly towards people who are not in the group.

daunting ADJ Something that is **daunting** makes you feel slightly afraid or worried about dealing with it. • *They were faced with the daunting task of restoring the house.*

contract N-COUNT A **contract** is a legal agreement, usually between two companies or individuals, which involves doing work or delivering a service for a stated sum of money. • *The company won a prestigious contract to work on Europe's tallest building.*

objective N-COUNT Your **objective** is what you are trying to achieve. • *His objective was to play golf and win.*

embrace VERB If you **embrace** a change, political system, or idea, you accept it and start supporting it or believing in it. • *He embraces the new information age.* **Embrace** is also a noun. • *The new rules have been embraced by government watchdog organizations.*

inclined ADJ If you are **inclined to** behave in a particular way, you often behave in that way, or you want to do so. • *Nobody felt inclined to argue with Smith.*

cycle N-COUNT A **cycle** is a series of events or processes that is repeated again and again, always in the same order. • *...the life cycle of the plant.*

purely ADV You use **purely** to emphasize that the thing you are mentioning is the most important feature or that it is the only thing which should be considered. • *The sportscar is a racing machine, designed purely for speed.*

left to your own devices If someone **is left to** their **own devices**, they are left to do what they want, or to look after themselves without any help. • *After tea we were* left to our own devices, so we decided to take a walk in the neighbouring village.

individualism N-UNCOUNT You use **individualism** to refer to the behaviour of someone who likes to think and do things in their own way, rather than imitating other people.

Unit 6

aerial cableway N-COUNT An **aerial cableway** is a moving cable which pulls a vehicle to transport people up mountains or steep hills. • *The peak is accessed by the longest aerial cableway in the Alps.*

inquiry N-COUNT An **inquiry** is a question which you ask in order to get some information. • *He made some inquiries and discovered she had gone abroad*

heritage N A country's **heritage** is all the qualities, traditions, or features of life there that have continued over many years and have been passed on from one generation to another. • *The historic building is as much part of our heritage as the paintings.*

point of view (points of view) N-COUNT You can refer to the opinions or attitudes that you have about something as your **point of view**. • *Thanks for your point of view, John.*

ferry N-COUNT A **ferry** is a boat that transports passengers and sometimes also vehicles, usually across rivers or short stretches of sea. • *They had recrossed the River Gambia by ferry.*

concession N-COUNT A **concession** is a special price which is lower than the usual price and which is often given to elderly people, students, and the unemployed. [BRIT] • *Open daily; admission £1.10 with concessions for children and OAPs.*

in AM, also use **reduction**

facility N-COUNT **Facilities** are buildings, pieces of equipment, or services that are provided for a particular purpose. • *What recreational facilities are now available?*

limited Something that is **limited** is not very great in amount, range, or degree. • *They may only have a limited amount of time to get their points across.*

access N-UNCOUNT If you have **access to** a building or other place, you are able or allowed to go into it. • *The facilities have been adapted to give access to wheelchair users.*

nature reserve N-COUNT A **nature reserve** is an area of land where the animals, birds, and plants are officially protected.

trail N-COUNT A **trail** is a rough path across open country or through forests. • *...a large area of woodland with hiking and walking trails.*

restricted ADJ Something that is **restricted** is quite small or limited. • *...the monotony of a heavily restricted diet.*

Unit 7

option N-COUNT An **option** is something that you can choose to do in preference to one or more alternatives.

category (categories) N-COUNT If people or things are divided into **categories**, they are divided into groups in such a way that the members of each group are similar to each other in some way.

penthouse suite N-COUNT A **penthouse** or a **penthouse apartment** or **suite** is a luxurious flat or set of rooms at the top of a tall building.

adjoin VERB If one room, place, or object **adjoins** another, they are next to each other.

commute See Unit 2 definition

pretty ADV You can use **pretty** before an adjective or adverb to mean 'quite' or 'rather'. • *I had a pretty good idea what she was going to do.* • *Pretty soon after my arrival I found somewhere to stay.*

Unit 8

available ADJ If something you want or need is **available**, you can find it or obtain it. • *The amount of money available to buy books has fallen by 17 per cent.* • *There are three small boats available for hire.* **availability** N-UNCOUNT

authorize VERB If someone in a position of authority **authorizes** something, they give their official permission for it to happen.

in BRIT, also use **authorise**

maintenance N-UNCOUNT The **maintenance** of a building, vehicle, road, or machine is the process of keeping it in good condition by regularly checking it and repairing it when necessary. • *The window had been replaced last week during routine maintenance.*

internal ADJ **Internal** is used to describe things that exist or happen inside a particular person, object, or place. • *Some of the internal walls of my house are made of plasterboard.*

appreciate VERB If you **appreciate** something that someone has done for you, you are grateful for it. • *Peter stood by me when I most needed it. I'll always appreciate that.*

Unit 9

performance N-COUNT A **performance** involves entertaining an audience by doing something such as singing, dancing, acting or showing a film. • *Inside the theatre, they were giving a performance of Bizet's Carmen.*

auditorium N-COUNT An **auditorium** is a large room, hall, or building which is used for events such as meetings and concerts. [AM]

debit card N-COUNT A **debit card** is a bank card that you can use to pay for things. When you use it the money is taken out of your bank account immediately.

key in PHRASAL VERB If you **key** something **in**, you type information into a computer or you give the computer a particular instruction by typing the information or instruction on the keyboard. • *Brian keyed in his personal code.*

automatic N-COUNT An **automatic** is a car in which the gears change automatically as the car's speed increases or decreases.

waiver N-COUNT A **waiver** is an official document that says a claim can be officially given up. • *He chose not to sign the insurance waiver.*

collision damage waiver N **Collision damage waiver** is a kind of insurance that you buy when you hire a car so that you do not need to pay if the car is damaged.

theft protection N-UNCOUNT If an insurance policy gives you **protection against** an event such as death, injury, fire, or theft, then the insurance company will give you or your family money if that event happens. • *The new policy is believed to be the first scheme to offer protection against an illness.*

insurance N **Insurance** is an arrangement in which you pay money to a company, and they pay money to you if something unpleasant happens to you, for example if your property is stolen or damaged, or if you get a serious illness. • *We recommend that you take out travel insurance on all holidays.*

third party ADJ **Third-party** insurance is a type of insurance that pays money to people who are hurt or whose property is damaged as a result of something you have done. It does not pay you any money for damage you suffer as a result of your own actions. [BRIT]

liable ADJ If you are **liable for** something such as a debt, you are legally responsible for it. • *The airline's insurer is liable for damages to the victims' families.* **liability** N-UNCOUNT • *He is claiming damages from London Underground, which has admitted liability but disputes the amount of his claim.*

component N-COUNT The **components** of something are the parts that it is made of. • *The management plan has four main components.*

comprehensive ADJ Something that is **comprehensive** includes everything that is needed or relevant. • *Before you go travelling in Nepal, be sure to read a comprehensive guide on the region.*

policy N-COUNT An insurance **policy** is a document which shows the agreement that you have made with an insurance company. • *You are advised to read the small print of household and motor insurance policies.*

supplementary ADJ **Supplementary** things are added to something in order to improve it. • *Provide them with additional background or with supplementary information.*

insure VERB If you **insure** yourself or your property, you pay money to an insurance company so that, if you become ill or if your property is damaged or stolen, the company will pay you a sum of money. If you are **uninsured**, you do not have this protection. • *For protection against unforeseen emergencies, you insure your house, your furnishings, and your car.*

excess (excesses) N-COUNT The **excess** on an insurance policy is a sum of money which the insured person has to pay towards the cost of a claim. The insurance company pays the rest. [BRIT] • *The company wanted £1,800 for a policy with a £400 excess for under-21s.*

quote VERB If someone **quotes** a price **for** doing something, they say how much money they would charge you for a service they are offering or a for a job that you want them to do. • *A travel agent quoted her £160 for a flight from Bristol to Palma.*

initial ADJ You use **initial** to describe something that happens at the beginning of a process. • *The initial reaction has been excellent.*

Unit 10

upgrade VERB If equipment or services **are upgraded**, they are improved or made more efficient. • *Helicopters have been upgraded and modernized.* **Upgrade** is also a noun. • *...equipment which needs expensive upgrades.*

to be after PHRASAL VERB If you are **after** something, you are trying to find or get it. • *If you're after a new bike, then we may have the model you are looking for.*

keypad N-COUNT The **keypad** on a modern telephone is the set of buttons that you press in order to operate it. Some other machines, such as cash dispensers, also have a keypad.

Wi-Fi N-UNCOUNT **Wi-Fi** is a mechanism to wirelessly connect electronic devices, such as a computer or a Smartphone, to the Internet. • *I access emails on my laptop via Wi-Fi.*

GPS N-UNCOUNT **GPS** is an abbreviation for global positioning system. **A global positioning system** is a system that uses signals from satellites to find out the position of an object.

app (apps) N-COUNT **App** is an abbreviation for **application**. An **application** is a small program designed for a mobile device.

denomination N-COUNT The **denomination** of a banknote or coin is its official value. • ...*a pile of bank notes, mostly in small denominations.*

Unit 11

westbound ADJ **Westbound** roads or vehicles lead to or are travelling towards the west. • ...*the last westbound train to leave Chicago.*

degree N-COUNT A **degree** is a unit of measurement that is used to measure temperatures. It is often written as °, for example 23 °. • *It's over 30 degrees outside.*

Unit 12

compulsory ADJ If something is **compulsory**, you must do it or accept it, because it is the law or because someone in a position of authority says you must.

logical ADJ The **logical** conclusion or result of a series of facts or events is the only one which can come from it, according to what makes sense. • *If the climate gets drier, then the logical conclusion is that more drought will follow.*

wood N-COUNT A **wood** is a fairly large area of trees growing near each other. You can refer to one or several of these areas as **woods**, and this is the usual form in American English.

overseas ADJ You use **overseas** to describe things that involve or are in foreign countries, usually across a sea or an ocean. • *He has returned to South Africa from his long overseas trip.* **Overseas** is also an adverb. • *If you're staying for more than three months or working overseas, a full ten-year passport is required.*

mind your own business PHRASE If you are **minding your own business**, you are doing the things that you normally do, without affecting what other people are doing. • *They were sitting at home, minding their own business, when it happened.*

Unit 13

stereotype N-COUNT A **stereotype** is a fixed general image or set of characteristics that a lot of people believe represent a particular type of person or thing. • *Many people feel their body shape doesn't live up to the stereotype of the ideal man or woman.*

temptation N-COUNT If you feel you want to do something or have something, even though you know you should avoid it, you can refer to this feeling as **temptation**. You can also refer to the thing you want to do or have as a **temptation**. • *Will they be able to resist the temptation to buy?*

Hispanic ADJ If somebody or something is **Hispanic** it means they or it come from Spain or a Spanish-speaking country, such as those in Latin America.

loan N-COUNT A **loan** is a sum of money that you borrow. • *The president wants to make it easier for small businesses to get bank loans.*

instalment N-COUNT If you pay for something in **instalments**, you pay small sums of money at regular intervals over a period of time, rather than paying the whole amount at once.

budget VERB If you **budget** certain amounts of money for particular things, you decide that you can afford to spend those amounts on those things. • *The company has budgeted $10 million for advertising.*

end up PHRASAL VERB If you **end up** doing something or **end up** in a particular state, you do that thing or get into that state even though you did not originally intend to. • *If you don't know what you want, you might end up getting something you don't want.*

against somebody's will PHRASE If something is done **against** your **will**, it is done even though you do not want it to be done.

set ADJ If you are **set to** do something, you are ready to do it or are likely to do it. If something is **set to** happen, it is about to happen or likely to happen. • *Roberto Baggio was set to become one of the greatest soccer players of all time.*

academic N-COUNT An **academic** is a member of a university or college who teaches or does research.

CV (CVs) N-COUNT Your **CV** is a brief written account of your personal details, your education, and the jobs you have had. You can send a CV when you are applying for a job. **CV** is an abbreviation for 'curriculum vitae'. [MAINLY BRIT] • *Send them a copy of your CV.*

in AM, also use **résumé**

compelling ADJ A **compelling** argument or reason is one that convinces you that something is true or that something should be done.

qualify VERB If you **qualify** for something or if something **qualifies** you for it, you have the right to do it or have it. • *To qualify for maternity leave, you must have worked for the same employer for two years.* • *The basic course does not qualify you to practise as a therapist.*

paradoxical ADJ If something is **paradoxical**, it involves two facts or qualities which seem to contradict each other.

frustrating ADJ Something that is **frustrating** annoys you or makes you angry, because you cannot do anything about the problems it causes. • *The current situation is very frustrating for us.*

bet N-COUNT If you tell someone that something is a **good bet** or the **best bet**, you are suggesting that it is the thing or course of action that they should choose. • *Your best bet is to choose a guest house.*

convince VERB If someone or something **convinces** you **to** do something, they persuade you to do it.

take a chance PHRASE When you **take a chance**, you try to do something, although there is a risk of danger or failure. • *You take a chance on the weather if you holiday in the UK.*

Unit 14

meticulous ADJ If you describe someone as **meticulous**, you mean that they do things very carefully and with great attention to detail.

thrown by VERB If you are **thrown by** something such as a remark or experience, it surprises you or confuses you because it is unexpected.

landscape N-COUNT The **landscape** of something is its features, characteristics and plans. • *The landscape of my week's travels changed when I fell and hurt my foot.*

up to speed PHRASE If you are **up to speed**, you have all the most recent information that you need about something. • *A day has been set aside to bring all councillors up to speed on the new proposal.*

up to PHRASE If you tell someone where you are **up to**, you tell them what stage you are at or how much progress you have made, for example with your work or with a book. • *I'm up to page 90 of this book.*

priority N-COUNT If something is a **priority**, it is the most important thing you have to do or deal with, or must be done or dealt with before everything else you have to do. • *Being a parent is her priority.*

deadline N-COUNT A **deadline** is a time or date before which a particular task must be finished or a particular

thing must be done. • *We were not able to meet the deadline because of manufacturing delays.*

vacancy N-COUNT A **vacancy** is a job or position which has not been filled. • *Most vacancies are at senior level, requiring appropriate qualifications.*

devise VERB If you **devise** a plan, system, or machine, you have the idea for it and design it. • *We devised a scheme to help him.*

performance review N-UNCOUNT A **performance review** or a **performance appraisal** is the process of judging the quality of an employee's work.

launch VERB To **launch** a large and important activity means to start it. **Launch** is also a noun. • *The launch of the new website took place on the designer's birthday.*

make sure PHRASE If you **make sure** that something is done, you take action so that it is done. • *Make sure that you follow the instructions carefully.*

drop the ball PHRASE If you **keep** a lot of **balls in the air**, you deal with many different things at the same time. If you **drop the ball**, you fail to do this. • *They had trouble keeping all their balls in the air. In management terms, they were trying to do too much and things were starting to break down.*

let something slip PHRASE If you **let something slip**, you allow it to get into a worse state or condition by not attending to it. • *We mustn't let our standards slip.*

implication N-COUNT The **implications of** something are the things that are likely to happen as a result. • *The low level of current investment has serious implications for future economic growth.*

vast ADJ Something that is **vast** is extremely large.

work out PHRASAL VERB If a situation **works out** well or **works out**, it happens or progresses in a satisfactory

way. • *Things just didn't work out as planned.*

get something right PHRASE If you **get something right**, you do it as it should be done. • *Get it right this time!*

diverse ADJ If a group or range of things is **diverse**, it is made up of a wide variety of things. • *...shops selling a diverse range of gifts.*

on location PHRASE A **location** is a place away from a studio where a film or part of a film is made. • *We're shooting the art film on location.*

shoot VERB When people **shoot** a film or **shoot** photographs, they make a film or take photographs using a camera. • *He'd love to shoot his film in Cuba.* N-COUNT **Shoot** is also a noun. • *...a barn being used for a video shoot.*

rectify VERB If you **rectify** something that is wrong, you change it so that it becomes correct or satisfactory.

enhance VERB To **enhance** something means to improve its value, quality, or attractiveness. • *They'll be keen to enhance their reputation abroad.*

complimentary ADJ A **complimentary** seat, ticket, or other item is given to you free. • *He had complimentary tickets to take his wife to watch the movie.*

Unit 15

enrich VERB To **enrich** something means to make it better or more enjoyable, usually by improving its quality. • *I believe that travelling enriches my appreciation of other cultures.*

exhaust VERB If something **exhausts** you, it makes you so tired, either physically or mentally, that you have no energy left. • **exhausting** ADJ • *It was an exhausting schedule she had set herself.*

detect VERB If you **detect** something, you identify or observe it. • *I didn't detect any regional accent.*

wind VERB If a road, river, or line of people **winds** in a particular direction, it goes in that direction with a lot of bends or twists in it. • *The Moselle winds through miles of tranquil countryside.*

monotone ADJ A **monotone** sound or surface does not have any variation in its tone or colour.

Unit 16

influence N-COUNT To have an **influence on** people or situations means to affect what they do or what happens. • *Van Gogh had a major influence on the development of modern painting.*

blog N-COUNT A **blog** is a website containing a diary or journal on a particular subject. **blogging** N-UNCOUNT • *...the explosion in the popularity of blogging.*

make sense PHRASE If a course of action **makes sense**, it seems sensible. • *It makes sense to look after yourself.*

ingredient N-COUNT **Ingredients** are the things that are used to make something, especially all the different foods you use when you are cooking a particular dish. • *Mix in the remaining ingredients before baking it in the oven.*

cockerel N-COUNT A **cockerel** is a young male chicken. [MAINLY BRIT]

open-mic night N-COUNT An **open-mic night** is an event usually held at a bar or club, where anyone can go on stage and sing, perform, or tell jokes.

gig N-COUNT A **gig** is a live performance by someone such as a musician or a comedian. • *He supplemented his income with occasional comedy gigs.*

a matter of N If you say that a situation is **a matter of** a particular thing, you mean that that is the most important thing to be done or considered when you are involved in the situation or explaining it.

Unit 17

concentrated ADJ If something **is concentrated in** an area, it is all there rather than being spread around.

cricket green N-COUNT A **cricket green** is an area of ground that is marked out and used for playing the game of cricket.

fete also **fête** N-COUNT A **fete** is an event that is usually held outdoors and includes competitions, entertainments, and the selling of used and home-made goods.

proceed N The **proceeds** of an event or activity are the money that has been obtained from it.

charity N-COUNT A **charity** is an organization which raises money in order to help people who are ill, disabled, or very poor. • *The National Trust is a registered charity.* N-UNCOUNT If you give money **to charity**, you give it to one or more charitable organizations. If you do something **for charity**, you do it in order to raise money for those organizations. • *He made substantial donations to charity.*

donate VERB If you **donate** something **to** a charity or other organization, you give it to them. • *He frequently donates large sums to charity.*

raffle N-COUNT A **raffle** is a competition in which you buy tickets with numbers on them. Afterwards some numbers are chosen, and if your ticket has one of these numbers on it, you win a prize.

coconut shy N-COUNT A **coconut shy** is a place at a fairground where people throw balls at coconuts on stands.

In the recording, the speaker calls this a 'coconut stall', but the standard term is 'coconut shy'.

scarecrow N-COUNT A **scarecrow** is an object in the shape of a person, which is put in a field where crops are growing in order to frighten birds away.

relay race N-COUNT A **relay** or a **relay race** is a race between two or more teams, for example teams of runners or swimmers. Each member of the team runs or swims one section of the race.

ride N-COUNT A **ride** is a journey on a horse, donkey, or bicycle, or in a vehicle. • *Would you like to go for a ride?*

stall N-COUNT A **stall** is a large table on which you put goods that you want to sell, or information that you want to give people. • *...market stalls selling local fruits.*

wellington N-COUNT **Wellingtons** or **wellington boots** are long rubber boots which you wear to keep your feet dry. They are also known as **wellies**. [MAINLY BRIT]

in AM, also use **rubber boots**

Unit 18

exercise N-COUNT **Exercises** are a series of movements or actions which you do in order to get fit, remain healthy, or practise for a particular physical activity. • *I do special neck and shoulder exercises.*

weightlifting N-UNCOUNT **Weightlifting** is a sport in which people lift weights to exercise, get fit or to compete with others.

aero-biking N-UNCOUNT **Aero-biking** is the use of special bicycles which do not move, so that you can exercise on them at home or at a gym.

mirror N-COUNT A **mirror** is a flat piece of glass which reflects light, so that when you look at it you can see yourself reflected in it. • *He absent-mindedly looked at himself in the mirror.*

treadmill N-UNCOUNT A **treadmill** is a piece of exercise equipment with a moving surface that you walk or run on while staying in the same place.

lane N-COUNT At a swimming pool or athletics track, a **lane** is a long narrow section which is marked by lines or ropes.

in proportion PHRASE If you keep something **in proportion**, you maintain a suitable amount of it. • *Tough decisions need to be made, but keep things in proportion and you'll avoid stress.*

posture N Your **posture** is the position in which you stand or sit. • *You can make your stomach look flatter instantly by improving your posture.*

slump VERB To **slump** means to carry your body with poor posture, forgetting to sit or stand up straight. • *If you are slumped all day at your desk, you can develop stiffness in your back and neck.*

vanity N-UNCOUNT If you refer to someone's **vanity**, you are critical of them because they take great pride in their appearance or abilities.

state of mind N-COUNT Your **state of mind** is your mood or mental state at a particular time. • *I want you to get into a whole new state of mind.*

cope VERB If you **cope with** a problem or task, you deal with it successfully. • *It was amazing how my mother coped with bringing up three children on very little money.*

Unit 19

cuisine The **cuisine** of a country or district is the style of cooking that is characteristic of that place. • *The cuisine of Japan is low in fat.*

pit N-COUNT A **pit** is a large hole.

coal N-UNCOUNT **Coal** is a hard black substance that is extracted from the ground and burned as fuel. • *Gas-fired electricity is cheaper than coal.* **Coals** are burning pieces of coal. • *It*

is important to get the coals white-hot before you start cooking.

extractor fan N-COUNT An **extractor** or **extractor fan** is a device that is fixed to a window or wall to draw smells, steam, or hot air out of a room. [MAINLY BRIT]

in AM, also use **ventilator**

ceiling N-COUNT A **ceiling** is the horizontal surface that forms the top part or roof inside a room. • *The rooms were spacious, with tall windows and high ceilings.*

self-conscious ADJ Someone who is **self-conscious** is easily embarrassed and nervous because they feel that others are looking at them and judging them. • *I felt a bit self-conscious in my swimming costume.*

veer VERB If someone or something **veers** in a certain direction, they change their position or direction.

profess VERB If you **profess to** do or have something, you claim that you do it or have it, often when you do not.

bistro N-COUNT A **bistro** is a small, informal restaurant or a bar where food is served.

Unit 20

full-contact ADJ A **full-contact** sport is one in which players touch each other and have physical contact, for example rugby or American football.

tackle VERB If you **tackle** someone in a game such as hockey or football, you try to take the ball away from them. If you **tackle** someone in rugby or American football, you knock them to the ground.

mud N-UNCOUNT **Mud** is a sticky mixture of earth and water. • *His uniform was crumpled, untidy, damp and dirty, splashed with mud.*

score VERB In a sport or game, if a player **scores** a goal or a point, they gain a goal or point.

damage N-UNCOUNT **Damage** is harm that is caused to an object. • *The blast caused extensive damage to the house.*

reputation N-COUNT Something's or someone's **reputation** is the opinion that people have about them. If they have a good reputation, people think they are good. • *The stories about his gambling ruined his reputation as a respectable man.*

religiously ADV If you do something **religiously**, you do it very regularly because you feel you should. • *Do these exercises religiously every day.*

dynamic ADJ If you describe something as **dynamic**, you approve of it because it is very active and energetic. • *South Asia continues to be the most dynamic economic region in the world.*

Unit 1   Your family

A

1

1   no
2   three – 'all but one' of her four sisters
3   because this means that the grandparents cannot help with childcare. Also so that they could see more of their grandchildren
4   none
5   because it is different

2

1   proximity
2   grew up
3   childcare
4   both sides
5   only child
6   extended

3

1   kids
2   all but
3   immediate
4   a conscious effort
5   childcare
6   rely on

B

1

1   true
2   true
3   false – he has three uncles and two aunts

4   false – it's an unusual nickname for his uncle whose real name is Alexander
5   false – she remarried ten years ago, many years after she was divorced
6   false – he has become part of the family

2

1   immediate
2   remarried
3   twenty to fifty (20 to 50)
4   short for
5   the head
6   matriarch
7   marriage
8   single, remarried

3

1   actually
2   is not particularly big
3   a large number of
4   please don't misunderstand me
5   well known for
6   that is our view
7   a well-respected man

4

1   funny
2   gathering
3   matriarch
4   period [US] (full stop = UK)
5   dare to question
6   huge

Unit 2   Your home town

A

1

1   false – Tonya says that, unlike many American cities, Atlanta is very green and is known as 'the city of trees'
2   true
3   false – Tonya says that people rely heavily on their cars and that the rail system is not designed properly, so not utilized fully
4   true

2

1   really great
2   great job
3   forward-thinking
4   culturally
5   will take the rail
6   gotta (got to)

3

1 c, 2 d, 3 a, 4 b, 5 f, 6 e

B

1

1 a village
2 the south of England
3 the middle of nowhere
4 about an hour

2

1 village
2 countryside proper
3 woodlands

Unit 3   Your country

A

1

1 true
2 false – Australia has frightening animals but New Zealand does not
3 true
4 true

3

1 for the first time
2 a few lizards
3 Italian, Greek
4 advanced
5 traded
6 joined

4

1 d, 2 b, 3 e, 4 a, 5 f, 6 c

Unit 4   Housing and accommodation

A

1

Property 1
Number of bedrooms: 3
Number of floors: 2
Number of bathrooms: 1
Garden: Yes
Balcony: Don't know
Views: Don't know
Car parking: Don't know
Gated: Don't know

4 middle of nowhere
5 courage
6 where we are now
7 takes about
8 to the train station

3

4 is correct – he would ideally like to live in the middle of nowhere, the real countryside, but he and his wife need to be able to get to work so that would not be practical.

4

1 c, 2 e, 3 b, 4 d, 5 f, 6 a

B

1

1 false – Stella feels that you can't learn about the country from a distance
2 true
3 true
4 false – she recommends these places because they are important parts of Chinese history and they allow people to understand where Chinese people have come from
5 true

3

1 distance
2 changes
3 diversity
4 see these places
5 so karaoke
6 young

Property 2
Number of bedrooms: 3
Number of floors: Don't know
Number of bathrooms: 2
Garden: Don't know
Balcony: Yes
Views: Yes
Car parking: Yes
Gated: Yes

Property 3
Number of bedrooms: 3
Number of floors: 2
Number of bathrooms: 2
Garden: No
Balcony: No
Views: Don't know
Car parking: Don't know
Gated: Don't know

2

Prope rty 1
1   three-bedroom
2   brand new
3   south-facing
4   double bed

Property 2
1   flat
2   twenty-four hour
3   small balcony
4   underground car parking

3

1   Did you say
2   that's really interesting

3   how big were
4   those three

B

1

1   no
2   you would die – you would be overworked
3   people are buying more appliances (we can infer that there is less need for staff)
4   fix plumbing, carry out electrical work, repair appliances

2

1   household
2   providing employment
3   not designed
4   to dust
5   the more

3

1 f, 2 c, 3 e, 4 a, 5 b, 6 d

Unit 5   Adapting to local customs

A

1

1   true
2   true
3   false – her family is not in the UK, so one of the things she misses during festivals is having her family around her
4   true
5   false – it annoys her

2

1   best of both
2   to participate
3   celebrated
4   do miss
5   struggle
6   messed up

3

1 b, 2 e, 3 d, 4 c, 5 f, 6 a

B

1

1   two Spanish girls

2   understanding the housing contract – she says she found a house very quickly
3   she couldn't understand why Lisa was confused
4   to live in the country where people speak the language you're learning, and to embrace the culture

2

1   interact with
2   daunting
3   used to
4   was reading
5   get through them
6   colloquial

3

5   4   3   6   2   1

C

1

1   false – he says getting involved is too much pressure!
2   true
3   false – it's rare for Americans to drink tea in the office
4   false – they don't expect you to offer

2

1 continues
2 so inclined
3 don't drink
4 don't really make
5 you're left

Unit 6   Tourist information

A

1

1 true
2 false – it is not one of the top six but it *is* worth visiting
3 false – you have to book in advance
4 true

3

1 Okay.
2 Oh yeah, okay.
3 OK, they sound interesting.
4 Um, probably a bit of both, probably…
5 You have to book in advance?

B

1

1 It opens at 10 am and closes at 4 pm
2 £2 (two pounds)

3 Lorna's mum
4 No
5 Because of the hills and steps on the trails

2

1 £3 (three pounds)
2 family ticket
3 facilities
4 limited access
5 restricted
6 wouldn't be able to
7 discount
8 free entry

3

1 d, 2 a, 3 c, 4 e

Unit 7   Hotel information

A

1

1 one – because he wanted to speak to 'hotel reservations'
2 23 September
3 $175 (one hundred and seventy-five dollars)
4 on the top floor
5 he's attending a wedding

2

1 start date
2 twenty-fifth
3 $165 (one sixty-five / one hundred and sixty-five dollars)
4 with a king
5 Continental
6 seating area
7 kitchenette
8 connects

3

Some suggestions:
1 When would you be leaving?
2 Would you be hiring a car?
3 How would you like to pay?
4 Would you like a double room?
5 Would you be needing a family room?

B

1

1 true
2 true
3 false – it is connected to the city by a commuter train, not a subway
4 true
5 false – but the White House *is* within walking distance

2

1 closest
2 further away
3 sixty dollars
4 commuter train
5 around the corner
6 just let us know

3

These phrases were all used:
Do you have any advice…?
Okay, cool.
That sounds good.
That sounds great.
Thank you very much.
Have a good day.
Yeah, you too.

Unit 8   Staying in a hotel

1

1 false – she does not have a booking
2 false – she says she would like a double room, and she is given a room with an en-suite bathroom
3 true
4 true
5 true

2

1 just check
2 availability
3 en suite
4 included
5 your passport
6 two nights' stay
7 keep the credit open
8 taking authorization
9 room service
10 all done for

3

Nikki used these phrases:
Okay, so $250 per night?
I'll probably want to go with that.

That sounds good.
What does that mean?
Great, thank you.
Perfect.

B

1

1 false – she wants to move rooms, because the room is noisy
2 false – she is a light sleeper, but she does not mention using earplugs
3 true
4 false

2

1 just a little problem
2 wondered if, maybe
3 actually
4 don't suppose, is there
5 I'd appreciate
6 Thanks very much

3

1 b, 2 d, 3 e, 4 a, 5 c

Unit 9   Phone transactions

1

1 true
2 false – the running time is 139 (one hundred and thirty-nine) minutes
3 true
4 false – there are seats available at the front, middle, and back

2

1 brand new

2 performance time
3 more options
4 altogether
5 standard seating
6 (£20.70) twenty pounds seventy
7 your card
8 hash key

3

1 b, 2 e, 3 d, 4 a, 5 g, 6 c, 7 f

(B)

1

1   true
2   true
3   false – he says that it will be 'something like' a Hyundai Sonata
4   true
5   true
6   true

2

1   into account
2   intermediate

3   air-conditioning
4   unlimited
5   insurance, collision
6   theft
7   fully comprehensive
8   supplementary
9   excess
10 tank

3

1 j, 2 i, 3 e, 4 g, 5 a, 6 d, 7 f, 8 c, 9 h, 10 b

Unit 10   Face-to-face transactions

(A)

1

1   his current contract is about to expire
2   no
3   two
4   £25 (twenty-five pounds)

2

1   runs out
2   touch-screen
3   high-tech
4   user-friendly
5   download
6   familiar
7   find it much easier
8   reasonably cheap

3

1	contract	4	qwerty
2	GPS	5	touch-screen
3	Twitter™	6	upgrade

(B)

1

1   true
2   true
3   false – she is told that it's best to buy them now
4   true
5   false – she asks for a mixture of small and large denominations

2

1   that sounds good
2   The best time to buy would be now
3   Okay, that sounds good.
4   a mixture would be
5   That would be great

3

1	currency	4	sell
2	deliver	5	meeting
3	customer	6	bank

Unit 11   Announcements

(A)

1

1   upstairs in the cinema
2   switch off your mobile phone and take your seats
3   in five minutes
4   *X-Men: First Class*
5   boys and girls, i.e. children

2

1   now open
2   in ten minutes
3   a final call
4   please remember
5   opera
6   3 (three)
7   just about
8   take your seats
9   will be starting
10 five minute

B

1

1 b, 2 b, 3 a, 4 a, 5 b

2

1 will be calling, approaches
2 boarding, mind the gap
3 yellow lines
4 are advised, entrance areas
5 westbound

3

1 b, 2 c, 3 f, 4 a, 5 d, 6 e

C

1

1 true
2 false – it's going to be dry during the day but will rain at night
3 false – the wind will lessen later
4 true

Unit 12 School days

A

1

1 When you're four or five years old
2 When you're sixteen years old
3 You can go to college
4 When she was eighteen years old
5 No

2

1 you can choose   4 slightly
2 you're sixteen   5 a little bit longer
3 in my area   6 its own system

B

1

1 because his parents lived in Germany and moved around every two years
2 eleven years – from when he was seven to when he was eighteen
3 yes, he did
4 he preferred to stay at school, if there was a big group of them

2

1 boarding school
2 steady friendships
3 prep school
4 normal day schools
5 put on
6 did choose
7 those of us
8 whole place, minding their own

C

1

1 true
2 false – she does get angry
3 false – she says that she sometimes wishes she were a student
4 true

2

1 chatty   5 could be
2 keep that   6 whereas
3 annoyed   7 appreciate
4 being

3

1 e, 2 c, 3 a, 4 b, 5 f, 6 d

Unit 13 Preparing for work

A

1

1 true
2 true (but she says it's just a stereotype, and that it's not necessarily true of all students)
3 false – she was social secretary of the Hispanic Society
4 false – she says 'it's not a huge amount of money'

2

2 4 8 6 7 3 1 5

3

1 a timetable   4 huge
2 a temptation   5 to budget
3 instalments   6 extra

B

1

1   English literature and Latin
2   the social side, and leaving home for the first time
3   more serious and focused
4   to become an academic

2

1   the social side
2   against

3   a little bit more
4   you wanted to be
5   set for

C

1

2   does not represent his thoughts

2

1   résumé
2   do have
3   a compelling case

4   qualify
5   paradoxical situation
6   best bet

Unit 14   Working life

A

1

1   no, it's varied
2   he 'clears' his emails – he goes through all of his new emails
3   true
4   next week
5   because the consequences for the organization are serious if the wrong person is selected

2

5   7   8   4   3   2   6   1

3

1   varied
2   thrown
3   upgraded

4   to achieve
5   different stages
6   critical

B

1

1   true
2   false – she says she supports various people, and she also leads a team of researchers
3   false – she often goes out 'on location'
4   true

2

1   a lot

2   content
3   support
4   go out
5   it

3

1 d, 2 a, 3 f, 4 b, 5 c

C

1

1   [in] the front office (the area where guests check in and check out, as opposed to working behind the scenes, with no contact with guests – this would be 'the back office')
2   In the morning when people check out, and again in the afternoon to evening when the new guests arrive.
3   bad check-in or bad breakfast experience
4   try to improve their stay by offering a room upgrade or a complimentary breakfast

2

1   all the people
2   guest comments
3   upset

4   rectify
5   enhance
6   exceeding

3

1 c, 2 a, 3 b, 4 d

Unit 15   Learning and using English

A

1

1   true

2   true
3   false – she says her ability really improved during her time on the Erasmus Programme
4   true

2

1 doing
2 made friends
3 have to think
4 accents
5 detect
6 much more precise
7 winding sentences
8 my non-native

3

5 6 4 2 3 1

1

1 when she was five years old
2 she feels comfortable
3 it's bad / funny!
4 she went to Canada twice on student exchanges and she is passionate about learning English

2

1 express myself
2 good education
3 particular accent

4 passionate
5 that much of a

3

Suggestions:
I feel comfortable
I love it
I'm passionate about it

C

1

3

3

1 You've never picked the accent.
2 I don't want to be in the shoes of somebody whom I don't know.
3 Speaking with their hands for sign language(s) and stuff.
4 I don't see it attractive.
5 If they don't hear me when I speak, that is different.

Unit 16   Hobbies and interests

A

1

1 her parents and grandparents
2 Spain and Italy
3 to share recipes and tips with colleagues
4 relaxed
5 when she needs to find an old recipe idea

2

Hannah mentions cooking pasta filled with meatballs and Spanish tortillas.

3

1 get together
2 pasta filled with meatballs
3 put them up
4 tips
5 download

4

1 b, 2 d, 3 e, 4 c, 5 f, 6 a

B

1

1 true
2 true

3 false – they don't seem to mind
4 false – they are thinking about it
5 false – they do have chickens, and that's where he got his cockerel from

2

1 the worst possible time of year
2 up and telling
3 did
4 gritted teeth
5 have to go

C

1

1 as much as possible (once a week)
2 because they all have full-time jobs
3 he rarely has time to go and see other bands play live
4 he would like to go to more festivals, gigs, and open-mic nights

2

1 once a week
2 try and practise
3 constantly
4 festivals or gigs
5 a number of
6 matter of

3

James uses these expressions:
once a month – they try to have a gig once a month
every week – a lot of bands play every week
every month – his band tries to have a gig every month

whenever I have spare time – he plays music whenever he has spare time
rarely have the time – he rarely has the time to go and see other people's live music
a fair bit of my time – music takes up a fair bit of his time

---

Unit 17 Socializing

A

1

1 false – Lisa says it's quite cheap
2 false – it's not necessary to have a plan
3 true
4 false – Lisa says that people usually don't wear coats on an evening out
5 true

2

1 famous
2 smallish city (see note on 'Largish' on page 11)
3 stereotype
4 I would always
5 are concentrated
6 makes sense

3

1 b, 2 c, 3 e, 4 a, 5 f, 6 d

B

1

1 on the cricket green
2 all the proceeds go to charity
3 the dog show
4 jams, breads, and cheeses
5 quite good

2

1	once	4	display
2	two pubs	5	donkey rides
3	all asked	6	bits and pieces

3

1 The plans had already been discussed (at the weekly meeting).
2 All of the proceeds were given to charity.
3 The organizer was presented with a large box of chocolates.
4 Fido was awarded the title of 'handsomest hound'.
5 The scarecrows had been made by the children (in their primary schools).

Unit 18 Keeping fit and healthy

A

1

1 one is for exercises and the other is for weightlifting
2 swimming lessons – children in the pool
3 from around 8 pm until closing time
4 some ID, such as a passport or a bill with your address on it

2

1	exercises	4	mirrors
2	weightlifting	5	treadmills
3	aero-biking	6	lane

B

1

1 true
2 true
3 true
4 false – he talks about trying to have good posture when sitting down at work
5 true

2

1	I should be eating	4	the amount and the times
2	finished your workout	5	lifts, stairs
3	wouldn't tell	6	posture, slumping

3

1 e, 2 c, 3 a, 4 b, 5 d

C

1

1 he wants to age well and he wants to maintain his physique
2 he wants to be able to kick a ball around and to go for family walks

3 no
4 he feels stress-free, relaxed, and energized

2

1 50 (fifty) years	5 stressful
2 let themselves go	6 going to the gym
3 vanity	7 automatic
4 start a family	8 release stress, cope

Unit 19   Eating in and eating out

A

1

1 because it smelled SO good
2 because it was upstairs and she wasn't sure what she would find and because she couldn't understand the menu
3 she found an app on her iPod which explained what to do
4 yes

2

1 so good	4 flavour
2 that's been cooked	5 a lot of fun
3 get with everything	6 each other

3

1 All the kimchi has been eaten.
2 The meat is usually barbecued for you.
3 The meat is wrapped in the lettuce leaf.
4 Is the salad often dressed with oil here?
5 Has the main course been cooked yet?
6 Is octopus ever eaten while it is still alive?

B

1

1 because Simon cooks
2 traditional Irish meals such as bacon and cabbage, stew and sweet and savoury salads
3 Yes
4 She does not think so.

2

1 veer off	4 profess
2 traditional	5 tend
3 savoury	6 try new things

C

1

3

2

6 4 5 1 3 2

Unit 20   Sport

A

1

1 false – you don't throw people to the ground. Instead you just 'touch' them
2 true
3 false – you touch your opponent with both hands
4 true

3

1 b, 2 c, 3 d, 4 a

B

1

3

3

1 for the winter holiday	4 ski resort
2 the skier's coming	5 on your own
3 managed	6 wouldn't be able to

C

1

1 he would watch every night, if he could
2 they feel very lucky
3 hockey is better, more dynamic, and more entertaining.

2

1 big sport	4 not popular
2 religiously	5 more dynamic, entertaining
3 snow or ice	6 falls down

TRANSCRIPT

The transcript below is an exact representation of what each speaker on the *Listening* CD says. No corrections or adaptations have been made.

Unit 1   Your family

Track 01

We don't— we don't really have any— any family <u>in close proximity</u>. So quite— of— some of my— My wife has quite a large family. She has four sisters. Um, all but one have kids as well, so our kids have an awful lot of cousins. Um, she has a couple of sisters who live not too far away so one about— down in Southampton, so about fifty kilometres (50 km) away, … um … one over in— over in London so— so similar … um … So neither of— neither my parents nor my wife's parents are close at all. My wife's parents are down in Cornwall, mine are up in Derbyshire where I— where I grew up. Um, so that, yeah, I mean that has been … um … It is— it is difficult, not having any <u>immediate family</u> that you can rely on for childcare. Um, it would be great if we— if we had, you know, either my parents or my wife's parents close by for the— for the childcare and also so that they could see more of the— more of the children as well… Um, we— we do, we make a <u>conscious</u> effort to— obviously to stay in touch with both sides of our family, so we'll go up to Derbyshire, my parents come down quite often.

Um, it's kind of— It was kind of interesting for me to become … um … part of my wife's family as well because I'm an only child. I don't have any brothers or sisters, so to kind of become part of this big <u>extended family</u> where there are, you know, … um … five sisters and twelve kids and… it's— is really great. Uh, you know, that was an experience that I— that I really enjoyed because I didn't— it was obviously different – not necessarily worse – but just different for me when I was— when I was growing up.

Track 02

Yes, I come from a very big family … um… in North Carolina … um … as families tend to go in North Carolina. My immediate family isn't— isn't so big. I have a brother and two stepsisters, as my mom is remarried. Um, however, my mother's family is huge. Um, she's one of six brothers and sisters – uh, the youngest, as a matter of fact – which means that all of her older brother and sisters … um … have loads and loads of children who also have loads of children. Yeah, uh … uh … I imagine we're anywhere from twenty to fifty for a normal family <u>gathering</u>, so if you can imagine that.

Well, they came out like a— like a straight-up *Brady Bunch* family. There are three— three boys and three girls. Um, the— the girls are called Glenda and Gail… um… who are my aunts of course, and my uncles are called Elec, David and Sammy, which— Elec is a very funny name … um … because— No one really knows why he's called Elec, because his name is actually Alexander, which— obviously <u>short for</u> Alexander would be Alex, but we just call him Elec for whatever reason.

Um, my grandma is definitely the head of the family … um … hands down. She's getting older, you know, getting on in her age now, but … um … is still definitely very much in charge … um … and no one would dare question anything that she says. But don't get me wrong, she's a— she's a very loving <u>matriarch</u> and everything, but her opinion is the final opinion on every matter, <u>period</u>.

Um, well yeah, my grandma was <u>divorced</u> from my grandpa … um … not an uncommon thing in the US. Um, I think we're pretty famous for divorce, just as much as we are anything else … um … but every good divorce always leads to a better marriage. I suppose that's how we look at it … um … and she was divorced … oh, just after my mom turned eighteen, I would imagine – somewhere right in there, and … uh … spent most of her life single and has recently remarried, probably in— in— within the past ten years. And her new husband is called Jack and is a really good guy … um … and immediately has become part of the family and…

Unit 2   Your home town

Track 03

Atlanta, Georgia is a really great city. It's … uh … often called the city of trees. Something that … um … we're really good at in the States is, when a city is being developed, taking all the trees out – just <u>bulldozing</u> them. Um, in Atlanta I think we've done a great job of maintaining the greenery in our city. Um, it is a <u>forward-thinking</u> city. There— Something interesting about Atlanta is there are— gosh, I think we're over six million in the metropolitan area, most of which did not grow up, obviously, in and around Atlanta. So we're a city of transplants, which makes us <u>culturally diverse</u> and … um … really very interesting.

In Atlanta we <u>rely on</u> our cars, too much actually. There is a rail system. Unfortunately, either it was not designed properly or people have just moved from— from where they were when that rail system was designed, so it's not fully utilized. I know a few people who will <u>take the rail</u> into work but not— We need to do something about that, because we have horrible traffic problems. It's not uncommon for someone to spend an hour each way into work when they're not really travelling that far, so we— we've gotta do something about transportation. I— I drive my car to and from my office. My office is less than ten miles from my house. So I'm on surface streets.

Track 04

Um, we live— I live with my— my family – wife and— and two kids … um … in a— in a village – a— a largish village, probably, ooh, I don't know, probably around three thousand (3,000) people – something like that, so a largish— a largish village … um … outside of a fairly large town. So you wouldn't— you wouldn't really call it, kind of, countryside <u>proper</u>. Um, there is a large amount of <u>common land</u> and woodlands that you can go in, you can take your bike out and go mountain biking, you can go for— you can go for walks, but you wouldn't— you would never feel that you were in the middle of nowhere, as you might do if you were in Scotland or if you were in the Lake District. Um …

I— I— I guess we live there partly just— just simply by the… It wasn't really a <u>conscious</u> decision to kind of move out of London. Um, that's always where I've lived since I moved down to the— to the South of England. I've always lived around that area. Um, it's somewhere where you can <u>commute</u> into London if you— if you need to. So I think … um … in our hearts, we'd probably quite like to live in the middle of nowhere in a really <u>rural</u> location, but we've never … um … I suppose had the … um … had the— the courage or the— or the jobs to allow us to, kind of, make that break. And the great— the great thing about where we are now is we can … um … as I do at the moment, I drive into— I drive into the— sort of West London which takes about, you know, about an hour. Or you can drive to the train station and be in the centre of London in half an hour, on— on the train.

Unit 3   Your country

Track 05

Australia and New Zealand are quite different, even <u>terrain</u>-wise. In particular, I was amazed when I went to Australia for the first time, 'cos I too was expecting it to be quite similar. Um, New Zealand's very <u>lush</u> and green. Um, Australia is quite red and the trees aren't very bushy, so it's all the eucalyptus trees rather than— New Zealand's got … um … bushy trees with lots of birds and insects, but no scary animals. And Australia is— looks more barren … uh … but it's really beautiful as well with the eucalyptus trees and… Their animals are more ferocious and they've got spiders and snakes and koalas and wallabies … um … but New Zealand just has the birds and a few lizards.

Australia's got a lot of— a large Italian community and Greek community. Uh, New Zealand is basically all made up of immigrants from the UK. There's quite a lot of Asians in later year that have come from Japan and Malaysia … um … and more so India now. But when I was growing up, it was a lot— a lot more just Europeans from the UK and…

The indigenous people in Australia have been there for a very, very long time and have lived in the desert for a long, long time. And I don't think had … um … encountered anybody for a long time until Europeans went there.

Uh, the Maori people travelled from somewhere. I don't think anyone knows exactly where, but I think it's... sort of thought that it's from Hawaii. And they travelled over in boats … um … and they were— they fought a lot amongst themselves so they were more advanced at <u>warfare</u> than the … um … <u>indigenous</u> people in Australia, as well. And they communicated a lot differently and they traded and… So I think, them as people as well as what happened to them after Europeans arrived in their land, differs. So the history seems to be quite different in both countries. And it is still a two and a half hour flight from New Zealand to Australia. They're not joined.

Track 06

I think, you know, the thing— It's, you know— You cannot learn about China from a distance. You need to come because, you know, it's a very big difference in cultures with the— the Western world, you know, in terms of the people, the place, you know, the— the history et cetera. So, I mean, when people came, you know, I think there are things that you can show to them. It's, you know, like shopping is a good way, 'cos they can see the changes in shopping. In the past, you can hardly see any luxurious good, but now it's— all the brands are there. You can also see some, you know … um … China make the cool, cheap goods, you know, that good— goods that you can buy at the very cheap prices. It's— it's there, you know, it's a— a city of variety and … um … diversity as well, you know. And you—we'll took them to see some history of China, like you know, to see the Forbidden City, the Great Wall, because this is what the heritage of China. You need to see these places. Then you can understand the Chinese history, you can understand why people— Chinese people— where they came from and why they— they are thinking, their <u>mindset</u> is like this, is different from the others, you know.

The other things that we can … um … you know, usually we can took them is like to karaoke. So karaoke's the place that, you know, they can say, 'Okay, this is what modern China people, you know, enjoy, going there, you know, have fun and gathering.' It's not only for young people, it's for everyone…

Unit 4 Housing and accommodation

Track 07

Estate agent	I— I've— I've got two options available. I've got one that's a three-bedroom house … um … on Parfrey Street … uh … which is located just … uh … five minutes' walk from here, quite close to the <u>tube</u> station, … um … close … uh … to the river. Um, it's a three-bedroom house over two floors, … uh … double reception, … uh … large eat-in kitchen. Uh, it's recently <u>refurbished</u>, so it's got a brand new kitchen in there … um …, new bathroom. Um, the rear garden is south-facing, so obviously you'll get the sun most of the day. Um, or th— there's two good-sized double bedrooms. The third one's obviously a bit smaller … um … but it's still large enough to fit a double bed and a wardrobe. Um, it's yeah, as I say, in pretty good order … um … and it's available from the— the twenty-second (22nd) of August. Um, what sort of date is it that you're looking to move?
Lizzie	Uh, as soon as possible, really.
Estate agent	As soon as possible. So, that— that could work. Would you like a <u>viewing</u> of it? Would you like to see…
Lizzie	Uh, did you say there was another <u>property</u>?
Estate agent	There— I've got another property which is— it's not a house, but it's actually a riverside … uh … flat … um … so it's three bedrooms again, two bathrooms, both … uh … — one en suite and … uh … and a separate cloakroom, … um … fairly n— large kitchen. Um, it's a <u>gated</u> development with twenty-four hour <u>porterage</u>. Um, obviously you get river views, there's a small balcony … um … that overlooks the river. Um, it's got an underground car parking space with it. Um, and that's available at the end of August.
Lizzie	Right, that's really interesting. Um, just out of interest, are there any flats in the area, apart from that one?

Estate agent	Uh, I've got a three-bedroom <u>maisonette</u> which is on … um … Lochaline Street that … uh … is a little bit smaller than— than the house. That's on the market at five hundred pounds (£500) per week. Um, it … uh … it is in … uh … fairly good order. Um, it was refurbished about five years ago … um … – maisonette being— meaning that it is over two floors. Um, there's two bathrooms there … uh … one of them is en suite. Um, the kitchen is fairly small … um … and there's no outside space with it, there's no garden.
Lizzie	And how big were the bedrooms in that one?
Estate agent	Uh, they're both good-sized double bedrooms, so big enough for, you know … They've actually both got built-in wardrobes … um … big enough for double beds. And, as I say, one of them's got an en-suite bathroom.
Lizzie	For those three, were they <u>furnished</u> or unfurnished, part-furnished?
Estate agent	Uh, they're actually, uh … Two of them are fully furnished, so everything is included … uh … even down to TVs and DVD players. Um, the other one is part-furnished, but the landlord is open to … uh … putting more … uh … furniture or TVs et cetera in there if— if you want them, so …

Track 08

You have household help. You have somebody to cook for you and wash your— A lady will come in the morning to wash your clothes and … uh … you know, you'll have somebody to do the cleaning for you. But it's not just about— In India, it's not just about having the help. It's not a luxury. It's also a means of providing employment to somebody. So it's a— it's— it serves two— two-fold purpose. And secondly, the houses in India are not designed for self-maintenance. You would die if you had to clean and scrub every day. Most— Majority of India is quite hot and the— just the scrubbing and the cleaning would take … You know, you need to dust every day. Here, you don't really need to dust every day, but in India you need to dust maybe twice a day. So … uh … it's the sheer volume of work as well, but … uh … I— I do find after having children that it's a lot more, 'cos I'd rather be with them rather than do housework and I guess as a working mum it's never the right balance. But in India, it is changing in the cities in the sense that people are getting dishwashers and washing machines and they just find it easier. Because the— not to forget, the more help you have, the more people you have to manage. But I think, by and large, that culture will not change of having household help.

So in India, you know, as a family, you would have a local handyman or somebody who comes round to fix your <u>plumbing</u> or your electricity or your refrigerator or any <u>appliance</u>. Or if something breaks, you would just give it or send it off to them and they would try and fix it.

Unit 5   Adapting to local customs

Track 09

Yeah— uh— it's— I mean— I find it easy to be— It's— it's quite nice to be an Indian in the UK, because in some ways we get the best of both worlds. We're able to enjoy our culture and do the, you know, Indians are quite religious. So we have a place of worship where we live … um … I'm a Sikh, so we have a Sikh temple where we live and we go and participate. We try and go there regularly to— … uh … on weekends to participate in the community gathering. And on festivals it's nice because there's a large enough Indian population in the UK for it to be a ce— celebration. I think Ken Livingston made, you know … um … one of our major— one of our Sikh New Years is actually celebrated in Trafalgar Square every year in the spring. It's called Vaisakhi. So he— he made a— he— he, I think he— he really … uh … really took a step— went a step further in trying to <u>integrate</u> and— and that's great, it's— What I do miss is not having family around to enjoy it with … uh … so it gets a bit lonely sometimes.

And then in terms of language, it can be a struggle because we are trying to teach our children our language, Hindi or Punjabi, and we find that a struggle because we speak very mixed languages with each other. We speak Hindi, Punjabi, English we throw in. It's— it's a complete mixed bag. So they're growing up a little bit messed up as well. I try and <u>enforce</u> the rule with them, but they just answer— Well, the younger one is too little, but ... uh ... my older one just answers me back in English and then I really have to force her to repeat it. And then she repeats it in a totally British accent and ... you know, that's— n— <u>no offence</u>, but that really does upset me.

Track 10

When I went to Spain, I thought it was important that I lived with Spanish people, so that I didn't just speak English all the time and stay w— I did know some people who were going to Madrid as well and— and so that I didn't just stay with them and form a <u>clique</u> and not ... um ... interact with the Spanish people. Um, so I lived with two Spanish girls which was <u>daunting</u> at first ... um ... but we got on really well and ... in the beginning they used to speak really slowly and loud ... um ... to make sure I would understand and I often felt like a bit of an idiot. Um, but soon they realized that I could understand— even though sometimes I might not know what to say in response, I could always ... um ... understand what they were saying.

I think the most difficult thing when I first arrived in Spain was... I found a house really quickly, but it was really hard to sort out the contract. I didn't understand the <u>contract</u> at all, 'cos it was all legal terms and really formal language. So that was really difficult ... um ... and my landlord— landlady was about eighty-five years old so she didn't speak any English. Um, she didn't really understand why I couldn't understand what I was reading and that was quite difficult. But I think those are the kinds of challenges you ha— you face when you move to a new country and they're things that you don't think of before you go, but you have to get through them when you're over there.

Obviously, th— the ... um ... the <u>objective</u> of your year abroad is to live in the country where they speak the language you're learning, <u>embrace</u> the culture, ... um ... you know, just talk to locals and learn as much— as many colloquial phrases ... um ... and, you know, things that people really say, instead of just things that you learn from textbooks and from your classes at university.

Track 11

Jeremy	And the tea culture here ...
Kara	Yes!
Jeremy	...is very different than in America. Here you s— you come into the office, about fifteen minutes into your day and you're already getting asked if you want a cup of tea, you know? And then it continues throughout the day. You could drink up to five, maybe eight cups of tea in a day if ... uh ... if you were so <u>inclined</u>. And then you've gotta make tea for everyone else. I mean— I'm— sometimes I just pretend I don't drink tea, because it's just too much pressure for me to— you know, to get involved in this— this tea <u>cycle</u>.
Interviewer	So— so what do— what do you do when you're back in the States? You don't drink tea?
Kara	Coffee purely...
Interviewer	Just coffee?
Jeremy	Just coffee.
Kara	... <u>purely</u> filtered coffee. A pot in the morning by myself and...
Jeremy	Yeah, you don't really make it for other people and people don't expect— expect to make it for you either. You're on your own.
Kara	No, and nobody will ask you if you want... They're getting a cup of coffee, 'Would you like anything?'
Jeremy	Yeah, it doesn't happen there.
Kara	No, no never.
Interviewer	So you just get your own— you just get your own coffee?
Kara	You just get your own coffee and you... everyone else gets their own. You're <u>left to your own devices</u>.
Jeremy	Yeah, you're on your own.

Kara	But it's not impolite.
Jeremy	Individualism!
Kara	Um, it's not considered impolite. It's just, you know…

Unit 6   Tourist information

Track 12

[phone rings]

Jessica	In Cape Town, we have our— the— the 'big six' which are the top six attractions …
Celia	Okay.
Jessica	…you know, in the— in— in the Cape Town area and those top six would include … um … your Cape Point which is … um … you know, a little bit in the south and then you also have, for example, your Kirstenbosch Botanical Gardens, … um … the V and A Waterfront, the Constantia winelands, Table Mountain <u>aerial cableway</u>, as well as also Robben Island. Okay, so…
Celia	Oh yeah, okay.
Jessica	… those would be the top attractions in Cape Town. The other ones that I can also add which, you know, we don't get— which doesn't get as … um … many <u>inquiries</u> or which are not as popular, you know, would be, for example, also the Castle of Good Hope which is the oldest building in Cape Town, as well as also the South African Museum. So those would be some of the must-see attractions that I would recommend you to see when you do come into Cape Town.
Celia	Okay, they sound interesting.
Jessica	Uh-huh. Um, it does also depend on what your preferences are, Celia. For example, if you are somebody who's more into culture and <u>heritage</u> as well as also maybe into, you know, outdoor activities … um … um…
Celia	Um, probably a bit of both, probably a mix, fro— fro— from my <u>point of view</u>. Um, uh … Ro— Robben Island … um … do you have to take a boat to that? I think I've heard— um, I think that some of my friends have mentioned this trip before and— and said it was amazing.
Jessica	Yes… Yes, it absolutely is, Celia. It's one of our top attractions in, you know, Cape Town and … um … it's definitely recommended. Um, with Robben Island, you have to pre-book due to the fact that it's a very, very popular tourist attraction…
Celia	You have to book in advance?
Jessica	… and the tour itself— That's— yes, you have to book in advance. Um, the tour itself is about three and a half hours. You take a <u>ferry</u> ride to the island and back, as well as also a bus ride on the island.

Track 13

[phone rings]

Leon	Hello RSPB, Vane Farm. Leon speaking.
Lorna	Hi there. Um, I was wondering if you could help me. Uh, I'm planning on— on coming to the farm, possibly this weekend. Could you tell me— I'd like to know the opening times and how much it's going to cost to get in.
Leon	Okay. The centre is open from ten o'clock in the morning until five pm in the afternoon and the café is open until four o'clock in the afternoon. It costs three pounds (£3) for an adult to … uh … go onto the RSPB reserve … uh … with fifty pence (50p) for children and two pounds (£2) for <u>concessions</u>. A family ticket costs six pounds (£6). If anybody who's visiting us is an RSPB member, then entry is free.
Lorna	Oh right, that's great. Um, and so … um … I think m— my mum is a member. I'm coming with my family, my mum is a member and … uh … we're planning on bringing my grandmother, as well. Uh, she's in a— a wheelchair. Is there— A— Are there <u>facilities</u> for people in wheelchairs? Would it be okay? Would we be able to walk around a bit w— with her?
Leon	There is <u>limited</u> <u>access</u> for people in wheelchairs. There would be no trouble in coming into the centre itself or going up to the café, but…

Lorna	Uh-huh.
Leon	… obviously, because we are a <u>nature reserve</u> and there are <u>trails</u> that go up hills and down a number of steps, I'm afraid that … uh … some of the access would be <u>restricted</u> and your grandmother wouldn't be able to … um … uh … explore the entire reserve.
Lorna	Okay, but— but there are some areas, 'cos I think we just want to come for a walk around and— and have maybe a— a cup of tea and a scone … um … in the café. Uh, so if— if she could … uh … come that would— that would be great. Um, and— and sorry, did you say there is a— an OAP discount?
Leon	Yes, there is. Uh, as I said …uh … members are allowed free entry and OAPs can come in for two pounds.

Unit 7   Hotel information

Track 14

[phone rings]

Automated recording	Thank you for calling the Tabard Inn. To reach the hotel or hotel reservations, press one. To reach the restaurant or restaurant reservations, press two. To reach our special events department, press three. To reach— [*beep*]… I'll transfer you now.

[phone rings]

Receptionist	Tabard Inn.
Jeremy	Hi, so I'm thinking about coming to your hotel … um … in about six weeks' time.
Receptionist	Great, uh … what would the start date be for that?
Jeremy	Um, it's … uh … end of September, September twenty-third and I'd be checking out the … uh … twenty-fifth.
Receptionist	Okay, twenty-third to the twenty-fifth. And that's a single room you're looking for?
Jeremy	Well, I'd— I kinda— I wanna know the different <u>options</u> I've got available.
Receptionist	Sure, yeah, we have … uh … rooms … uh … w— with a double bed, and … uh … the— the starting rate is one sixty-five (165). And then rooms with a queen are … uh … one seventy-five (175) and larger rooms with a king are one ninety-five (195). And continental breakfast is included with all of those, and … uh … the rooms get larger, there's more of a seat— seating area in each of the <u>categories</u>.
Jeremy	Uh-huh. And … um … if— if I did decide to bring my girlfriend with me, … um … which I might, … um … do you guys have any s— suites available or anything larger than the single room?
Receptionist	Uh, yes. We have … uh … we have the— the <u>penthouse suite</u> available. That would be … uh … two fifty (250) and that has a king bed and a small kitchenette area and a— a living room space and that's on the top floor, it has a nice view of the city.
Jeremy	Okay, great. And … um … I— I'm gonna be going for a wedding, so there's gonna to be a lot of people staying in this hotel. Do you guys have adjoining rooms or … um …
Receptionist	We do. We have … uh … rooms that <u>adjoin</u>. Uh, one of them has two double beds and it connects to a— a smaller room with one queen and they share a bathroom together.
Jeremy	Okay, great.

Track 15

Jeremy	Okay, great, and … um … I haven't booked my flight yet, but … um … I was wondering, do you— do you have any advice on how to best get there from the airport?

Receptionist	Yes, well … uh …, if you're flying into— uh, Reagan National is the closest. You can take … uh … the metro— the— the subway right in from there. Um, other airports are … uh … Dulles is … uh … f— further away and a cab is probably the easiest. Uh, it's— it's about sixty dollars ($60) in a cab. And then … uh … Baltimore – Washington Airport is … uh … connects to a <u>commuter train</u> that you can take right into the— the main train station in town.
Jeremy	Okay, cool. And are you guys <u>pretty</u> centrally located, then, in DC – like, next to all the sights and everything?
Receptionist	Yep, we're in the … uh … Dupont Circle area. Uh, pretty— pretty central to DC. You can walk down to the White House. Uh, the metro is right around the corner, so that gets you pretty much anywhere else you need to go.
Jeremy	Okay, well that sounds good. Alright, thank you. I'm gonna have a think about it and once I've got all my flights and everything booked, I'll give you a call.
Receptionist	Okay, that sounds great and just let us know. Thank you very much.
Jeremy	Thank you.
Receptionist	Have a good day.
Jeremy	Yeah, you too.

Unit 8   Staying in a hotel

Track 16

Receptionist	Good evening, welcome to the hotel.
Nikki	Hi there, I … uh … don't have a booking. I wondered if … um … there was any chance you had <u>availability</u> this evening?
Receptionist	I'll just check that for you, madam.
Nikki	I'm looking for two nights, please, and I'm here with my partner, so a double room, please.
Receptionist	A double room for two nights, certainly. One moment. *[typing]* Yes, we do have availability for you this evening … and the rate will be two hundred and fifty dollars ($250).
Nikki	Okay, so two hundred and fifty dollars per— per night?
Receptionist	Per night, yes madam.
Nikki	Okay. Is that en suite?
Receptionist	Yes, it does have an en suite and it also has an English breakfast included in the rate.
Nikki	Okay, then I think, if that's alright, I'll probably wanna go with that, yeah.
Receptionist	Okay, certainly. What I'll need from you, madam, is just your… passport and also if you'd like to pay cash or card.
Nikki	Okay, well here is my passport.
Nikki	And yeah, I think I'll pay with— Yeah, I'll pay with credit card, please.
Receptionist	Okay, thank you very much for that. *[typing]* Okay madam, so that's two nights' stay, with breakfast included, for two people in a double room. Is that right?
Nikki	Yeah, that sounds good.
Receptionist	Fantastic. Would you like me to keep the credit open in the room for you?
Nikki	Uh, what does— what does that mean?

Receptionist	If you wish to charge anything back to the room, i.e. any room service, dinner or drinks at the bar, I can leave the credit open for you and you're able to do that.
Nikki	Oh okay, so if you don't leave the credit open, then…
Receptionist	I'll just be taking authorization just for the room cost which will be two hundred and fifty dollars per night, so I'll be taking five hundred dollars ($500) and I'll close the lines in the room. But if you wish to order any room service, I'll take an additional fifty dollars ($50) as authorization and you can order any drinks, dinner or room service to the room.
Nikki	Okay … um … yeah, that sounds good. Let's leave the credit open then, please.
Receptionist	Certainly, I'll do that for you. [typing] Okay, thank you, madam. That's all done for you now. Here is your room— room keys.
Nikki	Great, thank you. And where are the lifts?
Receptionist	The lifts are just located up the corridor, to the right-hand side. You're located on the fourth floor, in room four zero four six (4046).
Nikki	Perfect.
Receptionist	Can I help you with anything else?
Nikki	No, that's everything, thank you very much.
Receptionist	Thank you very much. Enjoy your stay in our hotel.
Nikki	Thank you very much, bye.

Track 17

Nikki	Hello.
Receptionist	Good afternoon. How are you?
Nikki	I'm fine, thanks, I'm fine.
Receptionist	Fantastic. What can I do for you today?
Nikki	Um, actually there's just a little problem with my room. The air conditioning doesn't seem to be working and it's— you know, it's really hot outside. So I wondered if you could maybe get somebody to have a look at it for me?
Receptionist	Certainly. What I can do for you, I can send up maintenance in the next ten to fifteen minutes and then fix that issue for you. Is that okay?
Nikki	Y— Yeah, I— I have to admit it's actually quite a noisy room as well, because of the road outside. I don't suppose there's any chance of me moving rooms, is there?
Receptionist	Certainly, I can have a look for you. One moment. [typing] Okay madam, what I can do for you— I can move your room right away. It's ready now for you. I've organised an internal room which faces the courtyard.
Nikki	Oh great, so then there won't be any road noise.
Receptionist	No, there won't be any road noise.
Nikki	Thanks. It's just that I'm quite a light sleeper, so I'd appreciate not having to worry about the noise outside.
Receptionist	And that was room four zero four six. Is that right?
Nikki	That's right, yeah.
Receptionist	Fantastic. Okay, that's all done for you now. Here are your new keys to the room. And the room number is four zero four five (4045) which is just opposite your room, so it's a short walk.
Nikki	Oh good, so I can move really easily.
Receptionist	Of course. Do you need any help with your luggage?

Nikki	Oh no, that's fine. I don't have that much stuff with me, no problem.
Receptionist	Okay, great. Is there anything else I can do for you today?
Nikki	No, that's it. Thanks very much for your help.
Receptionist	Okay, you're welcome.
Nikki	Bye.

Unit 9   Phone transactions

Track 18

Vue	Welcome to the brand new Vue booking and information line. Which service would you like – film times or ticket booking?
Lily	Film times.
Vue	Okay, say the name of the film you want, or say 'What's on?'
Lily	*Tree of Life.*
Vue	You've chosen *Tree of Life*, certificate twelve A (12a). The remaining <u>performance</u> time for today is six ten pm (6.10 pm). The film running time is a hundred and thirty-nine (139) minutes. I can text the performance time information to you at a cost of just twenty-five P (25p). Would you like me to do that?
Lily	No.
Vue	Okay, to book tickets or hear more options, just stay on the line. Right, would you now like to book tickets for this film?
Lily	Yes.
Vue	Right, so that's today at six ten pm. Okay, if you need to book a wheelchair space or you're booking for a large group, please press the hash key now. Okay, how many tickets do you need altogether?
Lily	Two.
Vue	Two? Okay. Is that two adult tickets?
Lily	Yes.
Vue	Right, in this <u>auditorium</u>, we have standard seating and VIP seats. Which would you prefer?
Lily	Standard.
Vue	Thanks. Please wait while I check availability for you. *[music]* Okay, that's fine. We have availability at the back, the middle, or the front. Where would you like to sit?
Lily	Middle.
Vue	In the middle. Okay, I'll just confirm the details for you. So that's two adult tickets in our standard seating for the six ten pm showing of *Tree of Life*, today. Okay, those tickets have been reserved. Vue Cinemas charge a card handling fee of seventy P (70p) per ticket, up to a maximum of four pounds twenty (£4.20) which is charged by Vue Booking Services Limited for processing your card payment. So the total cost will be twenty pounds, seventy (£20.70). Now we need your credit or <u>debit card</u> details. Remember you'll need to bring your card with you when you come to collect your tickets. Right, please <u>key in</u> your card number, followed by the hash key.

Track 19

| Car rental assistant | Let me have a quick look through. I'll see what's on the system and I'll see which I think is probably gonna be the best for you. [*Okay, that's great.*] Um, now… we're taking into account that your wife wants to drive as well, and with there being four of you with some luggage there, I'm going to suggest to you an intermediate-class vehicle. [*Uh-huh.*] Uh, it would be something like a Hyundai Sonata or similar, okay? So it's an intermediate-size vehicle, four doors, <u>automatic</u> transmission, with air conditioning. Now this specific vehicle |

will come with unlimited mileage on there, so you don't physically need to worry about how many miles you're doing every day. In addition to that, you've also got insurance that consists of <u>collision damage waiver</u>, <u>theft protection</u>, <u>third-party</u> <u>liability</u> <u>insurance</u>. Now technically, those are the three <u>components</u> that make up a fully <u>comprehensive</u> <u>policy</u> in the UK. [*Uh-huh.*] In addition to that, you're also getting <u>supplementary</u> liability insurance and <u>uninsured</u> motorist protection. Those have all got a zero <u>excess</u> on them, okay? I'm gonna <u>quote</u> you on a package which also includes the <u>initial</u> tank of fuel when you pick the vehicle up and the cost for any additional drivers as well, so obviously your partner … uh … can drive at no extra charge with that. Now the price on that vehicle … um … for the eight days is coming in at two hundred and twenty-three pounds and eighty-seven pence (£223.87). How does that sound?

Freddy	In total? Or per day?
Car rental assistant	Two hundred and twenty-three pounds and eighty-seven pence in total, for the duration.
Freddy	Th— that sounds really good. And I can pick it up at San Francisco and drop it at Las Vegas?
Car rental assistant	Absolutely, at no extra charge. So, I— I can book this for you right now…

Unit 10   Face-to-face transactions

Track 20

Salesman	Hi.
Sam	Hi.
Salesman	Can I help you?
Sam	Yeah. Um, I'm looking for a new phone. The— the contract on my current phone runs out pretty soon [*Okay.*] and … uh … I'd like to <u>upgrade</u>.
Salesman	Okay. Um, what kind of phone are you after? Are you <u>after</u> like a … touch-screen phone or a qwerty-keypad phone or…
Sam	Well, I definitely want a phone that has the Internet, my— well, has 3G Internet. My current phone isn't particularly high-tech … um …, [*Okay.*] but I'm not really sure about maybe a touch-screen phone? I think I'd find the touch-screen quite hard to use. [*Okay.*] So perhaps something with … uh … like a qwerty <u>keypad</u>.
Salesman	Sure— I mean, I'll show you a touch-screen phone at the same time. [*Okay.*] Uh, there's two different phones, as you can see right in— in front of you. [*Yeah, yeah.*] Phone A, for example, [*Yeah.*] this one. [*Yeah.*] Um, it's got touch-screen phone. [*Oh yeah.*] Um, I mean it's quite … uh … user-friendly. [*Uh-huh.*] Uh, it's got <u>Wi-Fi</u>, it's got <u>GPS</u> on there. So let's just say you drive, this comes in handy for you.
Freddy	Okay, yeah, that'd be good.
Salesman	Um, and you can download all sorts of different <u>apps</u>, for example like Facebook™, Twitter™, and things like that, [*Okay, yeah.*] … um … and different apps. Uh, on your left-hand side, the phone B [*Yeah.*] … um … does similar functions and it's got qwerty keypad. [*Yeah, yeah, yeah.*] So if you're not too familiar with … uh … for example … um … touch-screen phones, [*Yeah.*] by all means— [*Yeah.*] some people just find it much easier to use a qwerty [*Yeah, yeah.*] keypad and similar function, you know. At the same time, … uh … it's got push emails, it's got Internet, you got 3G function that you're looking for, at the same time. [*Yeah, yeah.*] Uh, I mean, both phones are quite good and reasonably cheap as well, so you can get them [*Yeah, okay.*] as little as twenty-five pound (£25) a month.

Track 21

Caroline	I would like to buy some currency, please.
Salesman	Okay.

Caroline	Um, I'm doing two trips. I'm doing a trip to Spain which is for holiday and then I'm going to America for business.
Salesman	Okay.
Caroline	Um, so could I have, maybe, four hundred pounds (£400) … um … equivalent for each currency?
Salesman	Okay, four hundred pounds, yeah? So, if you're going to America, you need to take US dollars.
Caroline	Right.
Salesman	So for four hundred pounds … um … I can give you … six hundred and forty-two dollars ($642). Yeah?
Caroline	Right.
Salesman	And if you're going to Spain, obviously you need to take euros, for which … uh … you need to— I can give you four hundred and forty euros (€440), for four hundred pounds.
Caroline	Okay. That sounds good. Um, as I'm going to … uh … the USA in a couple of weeks' time … um …, is it best for me to buy the— the US dollars now?
Salesman	Yes. At the moment, the pound is very strong so you might— you— you are— you— you get more dollars. Yeah? At the moment, the best time to buy.
Caroline	The best time to buy would be now. Okay, thanks.
Salesman	Yeah.
Caroline	Okay well, I'd like to go ahead and do that, please.
Salesman	Okay.
Caroline	Um, and for the— … um … for the euros, what <u>denominations</u> can I have?
Salesman	Well, we have two hundreds, hundreds, fifties, twenties, tens, and fives. So for four hundred, I would recommend you to take some small denominations. Let's say fifties and below, so that you can spend … uh … them i— i— in Spain very easily. They rather prefer small denominations in Spain, yeah?
Caroline	Okay, that sounds good.
Salesman	Yeah, okay.
Caroline	Thank you.
Salesman	And what about US dollars? You want the small denominations as well for that?
Caroline	Um, a mixture would be fine.
Salesman	Mix— mixture would be fine. That's fine.
Caroline	So, maybe…
Salesman	We can give you some twenties, tens, fives, and one dollar…
Caroline	Yeah, so, maybe two one-hundred dollar bills? That would be great.

Unit 11   Announcements

Track 22

Good evening, ladies and gentleman. Welcome to Riverside Studio. The cinema's now open for tonight's film, *Pan's Labyrinth*, starting in ten minutes please, upstairs in the cinema.

Ladies and gentlemen, this is a final call please for tonight's performance in studio two. Final call for studio two. Please remember to switch off your mobiles and take your seats. Thank you.

Good evening, ladies and gentleman. Welcome to Riverside Studios and welcome to *Tête-à-Tête*, the opera festival. Studio three is now open for tonight's performance of *The City Weeps*, starting in five minutes please, in studio three.

Good evening, ladies and gentlemen and welcome to Riverside Studios. This is a final call for tonight's film, *X-Men: First Class*, just about to start upstairs in the cinema. Please could you take your seats. This is a final call.

Good morning, ladies and gentlemen, boys and girls. This morning's performance by Hairy Maclary will be starting in five minutes in studio two. Please could you take your seats. This is a five minute call.

Track 23

Ladies and gentlemen, your next train on platform two is your <u>westbound</u> Piccadilly line, calling at all stations to Heathrow Airport. This train will be calling at Acton Town and then all stations to Heathrow, terminals four, one, two, and three. When this train approaches the platform, please make sure you stand behind the yellow lines. Let the passengers off the train first, before boarding.

Ladies and gentlemen, the next train on platform one is your westbound District line, calling at all stations to Ealing Broadway. When the train is approaching the platform, make sure you stand behind the yellow lines at all times. Let the passengers off the train first before boarding and mind the gap between the train and the platform.

Please make sure you stand behind the yellow lines at all times. Let the passengers off their train first, before boarding. So your next Richmond, two minutes, and your next Ealing Broadway, approximately four minutes.

Ladies and gentlemen, you are advised to use the whole area of the platform. Keep away from the exit and the entrance areas. Move right along the platform and use all available space.

Ladies and gentlemen, your next train on platform two is your westbound Piccadilly line, calling at all stations to Heathrow Airport, calling at Acton Town, then all stations to Heathrow, terminals five, and one, two and three. When the train does arrive, let the passengers off the train first, before boarding. And move right inside the carriages and use all available space. Next train on platform two, all stations Heathrow.

Track 24

A mostly sunny day with winds increasing to forty kilometres per hour (40 kmph) tonight. A forecast top, twenty-two. Tomorrow, dry with some rain at night, twenty-two. Friday, areas of rain, seventeen. On the bays, a strong wind warning is current, northerlies to thirty knots then easing later. Waves at one to one and a half metres (1½m). At Sydenham – fifteen; Boronia – sixteen; the city – it's fifteen <u>degrees</u> (15°). David Armstrong, Melbourne's own, 3AW.

Unit 12   School days

Track 25

In England and Wales, usually you attend primary school from about four or five till ten or eleven and then you attend high school from being eleven until you're sixteen. Um, that's your <u>compulsory</u> education and then you can choose to stay— If your school has a sixth form, you can choose to stay till you're eighteen or you can go to college when you're sixteen and get the same qualifications. Um, a lot of schools in my area don't have a sixth form, which is part of the reason that I went to the school I did. But … um … because mine did, so I was at school— at my high school from the age of eleven to eighteen.

Um, schools in Scotland are slightly different. In England and Wales, you go to school a little bit longer than you do in Scotland. Um, I went to high school for seven years … um … and if I was in Scotland, I would have gone for six years and then gone to university. Um, and then Northern Ireland has its own system, so that's different to England and Wales and Scotland.

Track 26

I went to boarding school from the age of seven. Um, my parents lived in Germany at the time, so it was the <u>logical</u> thing to do. They were moving around every two years … um … so the best thing for me was to— … um … to go and have steady friendships … um … at— at one school. Um, so I— I went when I was seven, as I said, and … um … up until the age of eighteen. Uh, I was at a prep school from seven till fourteen and then I went to college until I was eighteen. Um, I suppose it— the main difference obviously is that it— … uh … for— to— … uh … to normal day schools is that I was at— … um … I was at school most of the time, I would stay there. Uh, we would occasionally be let out on— o— on the weekends … uh … and for half term. Um, and generally it was a very fun place to be, … um … because you're spending all your time with your friends and your parents are nowhere near you. But … uh … but yeah, generally it— it's great. There … um … there were quite a few activities put on for us. There were— there were sports hall facilities, swimming pool. Um, there were <u>woods</u> you could play in … um … and … uh … and yeah, just lots of— lots of sport to do, lots of— … um … lots of weekend activities. So I mean there was— there was loads to do. Um, and yeah, it was just a really good, fun time on the whole.

A lot of the boys did choose to go home … um …quite often if— if their parents could have them and— and … um … most— yeah, most people had parents who lived in … um … nearby towns or— or in London, so— so not too far away. Um, that was quite good fun for— for those of us who ha— had parents living <u>overseas</u>, because we could just go and stay with— with friends … um … uh… in— in nicer parts of the country. Um, but … um … it was actually more fun I think when— when you had a big group of people that stayed in for a weekend and— and you had the whole place to yourself and all the teachers were sort of quietly <u>minding their own business</u>.

Track 27

Has it been strange going back to teach at school … uh … when I'm not that long away from being a student myself? Um, yeah, I think it's been quite strange, and particularly with the older ch— … um … years that I teach, I have not felt, you know, incredibly mu— you know, older than them. And therefore, there's a sort of relationship where you almost want to, kind of, be more chatty with them and have a bit of fun, but you know you've got to keep that line.

Um, I would say that it— yeah, I mean, I— obviously, now that I'm a teacher, want their attention every second. And I'm a— I'm annoyed if they're not— you know, they're talking or if they're looking away or if they're looking at the clock and I'm just thinking, you know, 'This is my lesson!' So— But, I mean, I do remember school being very tiring. Um, and … I guess one of the main things for me is that, just occasionally in the morning when I'm on my way to s— when— on my way to school, I just think, 'Gosh, I wish it could be me that was … um … at— at the desk with— you know, just writing things down.' Whereas, you know, being the teacher is just so much work and I don't think I realised how much work it was, being the teacher. So I kind of now appreciate some of the teachers that I had, if that makes sense.

Unit 13   Preparing for work

Track 28

I think UK universities have a different focus, in a way, to universities in other countries, because often your timetable isn't that busy. You might only have twelve hours … um … of lectures or seminars a week, so you have a lot of free time. And in that free time, you're free— as long as you do your work, you're free to do whatever you want, so…

There's a <u>stereotype</u> that a lot of students just waste their free time … um … by sleeping till late, going out all night … um … like, four or five times during the week. There is a <u>temptation</u>, when you're at uni and you might only have ten to twelve hours of lectures a week, to just waste quite a lot of time, watch a lot of bad TV, … um… go out too much … um … but often students get a job. There are really good … um … societies and clubs at universities in the UK. Um, so that often takes up a lot of time. I was in the Ski Club … um … throughout uni and I was also the social secretary for the <u>Hispanic</u> Society.

So when you go to university in the UK, usually you take out a student <u>loan</u> … um … and this is a loan that you receive every year in <u>instalments</u>, so three times a year. Um, most students in the UK live on their student loan. It's not a huge amount of money. Um, people don't have a lot of extra money to spend on clothes and, you know, going out and going on trips and things. Um, but that's part of the experience, because you have to learn to <u>budget</u> what you have and…

Track 29

The number of universities I've been to? Well, I've— Uh, it— it— it— it differs obviously with the stage of your education. So my undergraduate degree, it— it was very much about the social side. It was about … um … leaving home for the first time. Um, I studied English Literature. Um, somehow <u>ended up</u> doing Latin as well, which was … um … <u>against my will</u>. Um, so that was one stage. I then went on to do a Masters at a different university which was … um … a little bit more focused, a bit more serious. It— It's— you— you were there because you wanted to be there. It was much more about the— … um … the discipline. Um, again that was in— … uh … studying literature – sort of highly … um … economically useful. Um, and then I ended up in … um … in Belfast, in Northern Ireland, doing a PhD. Um, so I was all— <u>all set for</u> a … um … career as … um … an <u>academic</u>. Um, and then it all— it all changed.

Track 30

When you're writing a <u>CV</u> or a résumé, when you— when you're doing it straight out of college, you don't have very many experiences that a lot of companies are gonna look for. What you do have is education, though. So I think that anybody who's coming out of university – that's the first thing that they need to put and make a <u>compelling</u> case for, is that they— they are well educated and that they did extremely well in school. Because most of the experience you'll have isn't really gonna <u>qualify</u> you for any of the work, which is kind of a— a <u>paradoxical</u> situation for first-time workers, is that everybody's asking for experience and you don't have any. So it's a very <u>frustrating</u> cycle. And… I— the— your <u>best bet</u> is just <u>convincing</u> an employee to <u>take a chance</u> by looking at the qualities you do have which … if it— you— if it's your first job, all you have is your time as a student.

Unit 14   Working life

Track 31

My day really is … um … quite varied ev— you— every day. It's … um … you know, you can come in and plan everything out <u>meticulously</u> and ultimately your day will <u>be thrown by</u> a manager coming up to you and asking you for a particular request which will change, you know, the whole <u>landscape</u> of what you're gonna face for the rest of the— the afternoon.

First thing I do when I come in is I clear all my emails, just so I can be up to— <u>up to speed</u> of where I'm <u>up to</u>. And then certainly I— I'm quite organized, so I like to do a list of the f— most important things that I need to— who I need to respond to and in what order. It's all about <u>priorities</u> and <u>deadlines</u>. So, I suppose a typical day is: I've got ten <u>vacancies</u> at the moment that I'm looking after.

And the other thing … um … that I've got is I'm <u>devising</u> a training programme for our <u>performance reviews</u> … um … 'cos we've just <u>launched</u> our online performance review. We've upgraded it, so I'm devising a programme that I can roll out next week. So they're the things I'd like to achieve … um … and in that— For— for instance, for ten vacancies I've got, I've got to make sure they're all tracking on time. So one of them— They're all at different stages –

one of them might be at, you know, advertising stage, one of them will be at final interview stage. So there's a whole mix of <u>making sure</u> you don't <u>drop any balls</u> in the process, 'cos you can't <u>let anything slip</u>.

You know, if you make a mistake at the hiring stage, you— you pay— the payback is really … um … Sorry, the— the … um … <u>implications</u> are so <u>vast</u> when someone joins an organization and they haven't <u>worked out</u>. So, it's, you know, the— the— it's so critical to <u>get it right</u>.

Track 32

My name is Anna Coppi and I'm a TV producer and no two days in my job are ever the same. My job role is very <u>diverse</u> and generally, on a day-to-day basis, I am office-based. I spend a lot of time speaking to people on the phone, researching. My main role is to provide content for a television programme. I support a director and other producers and I also lead a team of researchers. Often I can go out <u>on location</u> and work on <u>shoots</u> where I am using a film camera, directing what we call contributors. A contributor could be a presenter, it could be a person that is telling us about their skill, it could be a member of a family that we're filming with. I've worked with wrestlers and doctors and plastic surgeons and dog trainers and wedding co-ordinators. It's a really diverse role and very enjoyable.

Track 33

I work as a duty manager in a hotel. I work on the front office. My day-to-day basis consists of looking after the guests. Um, from the morning, it would be to check the arrivals and see how many people we have coming into the hotel, looking after all the departures in the morning, and preparing and planning for the day. Our busy times would be in the morning when we have our— all the people checking out of the hotel – all our departures. And then in the afternoon to evening, where all the people are coming in – all the arrivals for that day of the hotel.

In my job as well as a duty manager here, I look after a lot of the guest comments, feedback, and also complaints. So anything to do with a guest coming to the hotel that's upset or had a dissatisfied stay, I would then try to <u>rectify</u> that or, you know, follow that up to— to see what the guest— if there was a problem with their stay, if they've had a bad check-in or— or breakfast experience— For then myself, one of my duties is to follow that up, chase them, meet them, and see if … um … I can somehow <u>enhance</u> their stay for the next couple of days whether they— they're staying in the hotel then. So that could be possibly offering a— an upgrade to a room or <u>complimentary</u> breakfast or looking after them in any sort of general way, sort of exceeding their expectations...

Unit 15   Learning and using English

Track 34

When I was … uh … doing my Erasmus year in Leicester and I— I made friends with lots of … uh … in— different international people, and of course, we had to communicate in English. I would speak English to kind of get to know people and it was a very <u>enriching</u> and great experience to actually … um … develop a personality in a foreign language. Um, it's also— it's <u>exhausting</u> … uh … in a way … um … at first … um … to kind of like— always having to think about what you're saying a little bit more than when you w— you know, use your native language. Um, however, you know, you adapt very, very quickly and then you just— you know, the words just come out of your mouth and you don't really have to think about it anymore and you're just communicating in English – with a foreign accent which is still there and it's … um … still good. You know, you—you come from certain place and … um … your language rele— reveals that, so that's— that's great. So English was very, very important for me when I was in Leicester, 'cos that was kind of like the— the way to meet other people and … um … I got to know lots of different foreign accents … um … so my ability to, kind of, like <u>detect</u> accents and also to understand foreign accents really improved.

I always found that English is much more precise as a language … um …, especially when you write – um, English, you just go for it. You— you hit the point straight away, whereas in German you circle a point and then you come close and then you move away again. So German has lots of very long and, you know, <u>winding</u> sentences, whereas English is … um … straight to the point – short sentence, say what you mean a— and that's it. So I always appreciated English for that, I have to say. Um, and sometimes it was even difficult for me to write in German, because … um … I really enjoyed writing in English so much. So … um … it kind of turned around at a certain level … um … and I preferred writing in my non-native language, I— I suppose.

Track 35

Um, my mum made me learn English very early, when I was about, like, five, 'cos she thought it was pretty important. And I always enjoyed it, 'cos I think I can express myself more in English than in German. German is a very <u>monotone</u> language and English is more with ups and downs and you can— I don't know how to explain that, but … um … I feel comfortable in speaking w— English, so it's… I love it.

Everybody has to have it in high school, so I think we have a really good education, especially in English. But … um … most of them have a really bad accent. I can hear that when I … was working at the bar. I just knew that it— the guys were from Germany, 'cos they had those particular accent which is really funny. But … um … yeah, I don't really have an accent cause … uh … I went to Canada two times … um … for student exchanges and well, I'm passionate about English, so I guess I don't really have that much of an … German accent.

Track 36

I've been told by a friend that, 'You've been living in England, but you've never picked the accent.' And I'd say, 'Yeah!' Um, probably 'cos I don't want to be in the shoes of somebody whom I don't know. Yeah, so I prefer to … relax in my accent, 'cos when I speak, people hear. So I don't see why I should change it.

Yeah, it's become … um … I think a style people are adopting. Like the youth in my country would love to behave like Americans, with their jeans coming off and also speaking with their hands for sign languages and stuff. And I don't see it … um … attractive. And the person who will say, asking me about this, … um … even though he doesn't want his accent to be changed, but … um … he's seen so many people, spoken with so many people, who try to say 'Innit?' and those stuff. So whenever I speak to him and I don't say anything of that sort… So I guess that's the main reason why he said my accent hasn't changed, why haven't I tried to? If they don't hear me when I speak, that is different. Then you have to work hard to change your accent. But since they hear whatever I wanna say to them, I don't think I have a problem.

Unit 16   Hobbies and interests

Track 37

So when I've finished work and … um … I've got some free time or at the weekends, I absolutely love to cook. Um, it's a real family passion … um … and I think it's come not just from my parents, but also from my grandmothers and grandfathers. Um, and as a family, we really love to get together … um … and have big meals. And I think from living in different countries, um – so I spent some time in S— living in Spain and … um … another bit of time living in Italy – really brought all these different <u>influences</u> into what I love to cook. So whether it's a big pasta … um … filled with meatballs or whether it's tortilla from Spain, there's all sorts of things that we love to put on the table.

Um, and even now, I mean, I talk about recipes in the office with my friends. Um, I'm always, always going on about food and I'll be the first one to make a lunch or a dinner appointment, instead of going for a coffee. Um, and that has now spread to me making a food <u>blog</u> … um … in which I get the best recipes that I cook and put them up there, because I was always getting people from the office asking me … um … just the things I'd brought in for lunch, I mean, what the recipe was or we'd be sharing tips and I thought, 'Why not make it, so that people can – rather than me handing it to them on a scrap of paper or photocopying it – why not put it there, so that they can download it themselves?' Uh, I mean, it seemed to <u>make sense</u>.

I really enjoy the process of blogging. Um, not just because I like the sound of my own voice … um … but also because I think it— it's surprisingly relaxing. It's one of the things I really enjoy sitting down and doing in my spare time. Um, so the food blog that I have … um … I put up recipes, I put up photos and all those boring things that lots of people love to do. Um, and then I find myself, for example, at my boyfriend's house or at my grandma's and I haven't got the cookbook that I want with me or we've got a few ingredients in the fridge and I know I've got a brilliant recipe, but I haven't got it there. And I remember that I've put it— something on my blog about it and I can just go on, download the recipe, take the ingredients list to the shops and there, it's done.

Track 38

So we've got a— an area at the bottom of the garden where we keep a few chickens. The kids can go down and collect the eggs, which is a nice thing for them to do. Um, we just got a cockerel very recently so… Summer is probably the worst possible time of year to get a cockerel, because— because it's— it starts getting light this time of year about half past four. Then obviously, as soon as it goes I— it gets light, then the cockerel's up and telling everybody that he's up and awake and … um … yeah.

We did ask the neighbours if it was— if it was going to be a problem and they said, 'No, no, it's fine, it's fine,' but I think they had slightly gritted teeth when they— when they said that. So the cockerel may have to— may have to go back. He's actually— he's from my parents, because my parents keep chickens as a hobby as well, so that's where the cockerel came from. But, yeah, aside from that we may get a dog sometime soon, or possibly a cat, but at the moment we just have the chickens.

Track 39

Um, music takes up a fair bit of my time. I m— The band … uh … tries to practise once a week, if we can. We're all fairly busy – we have full-time jobs as well – but … um … but we do try and practise as much as possible. We try and … um … have a gig every month, if we can. Um, a lot of bands will play every week and— and just play to five people, but we think that's completely pointless. We're never gonna get anywhere like that, so we try and get … um … you know, a hundred people through the door if we can and— and just do it once a month, make it really big, make it a big event. Um, so yeah, I— I'm— I'm constantly listening to music and— and playing it whenever I have spe—spare time, really.

I would say I'm… very interested in going to see other people's live music, but it's something that I very rarely have the time for. Um, I don't go to enough festivals or gigs and I would love to go to more. Um, part of the reason for that is … um … is the cost of doing it. Um, having said that, there are a number of very, very good … um … open-mic nights and— and cheap nights … um … or free nights in— all around London. Um, it's just a matter of knowing where they are … um … and finding the time to do it and it's something that I would like to do more of.

Unit 17   Socializing

Track 40

Going out in Newcastle is quite— It's quite a famous place to … um … go for a night out and there's lots of hen-dos and stag parties … and, you know, girls' weekends away, because it's quite cheap to go out in Newcastle. Um, lots of bars are concentrated in one area, so you don't have to travel between the bars and there are lots and lots and lots of bars to choose from, even though it's a smallish city compared to London. I really like going out in Newcastle because you don't need to plan where you're going out. You can just go to one bar, the next bar is next door … um … and you don't have to walk a great deal. Well, Newcastle is in the North of England and it's not really the warmest of places … um … but there's a stereotype, I think around Europe, that people from Newcastle don't wear coats … um … or suitable clothing when they go out … um … even though it is quite cold usually, especially late at night. Um, and you will see lots of girls without coats wearing dresses and boys just wearing T-shirts, even though it's really cold outside. But I think that's part of the fun. And when I go out in London, I would always take a coat. But when I go out in Newcastle … um … if I take a coat, my friends from Newcastle say, 'Lisa, why do you have a coat on?'

Um, I wonder if people in Newcastle started not wearing coats because all the bars and all the places you want to go are concentrated in a small area. As long as you get to town okay and get picked up or get a taxi home, then you don't really need a coat because you're not outside so much. So in a way, it kind of makes sense.

Track 41

It was about three weeks ago, we had the village <u>fête</u>. It happens once a year in Shamley Green where I live. Um, it's a very small village. To give you an idea, we've got one shop and two pubs and a cricket green in the middle of the whole lot. Um, and the fête h— happens on— on the <u>cricket green</u>. So, you basically— it's— all <u>proceeds</u> go to charity and we were all asked as neighbours in the village to <u>donate</u> something for … um … the <u>raffle</u>, so … um … a bottle of whatever, a box of chocolates, box of biscuits, things like that. So, you have things like face-painting for the kids and <u>coconut</u> … um … <u>stalls</u>. And the dog show is always a winner! And … um … they had things like, you know, 'handsomest hound' – prizes for that and a— all these different ones. Um, also there was a display where the kids the week before in the primary school had made <u>scarecrows</u>, so there was a scarecrow judging competition from all the scarecrows from the school for that week. Um, also <u>relay races</u> with the kids and <u>donkey rides</u> for the children and, you know, the raffle – just various bits and pieces and a few <u>stalls</u> where you can buy jams and breads and, you know, cheeses, different things like that. But … um … I think all proceeds go to charity, so it's a good day out. It h— it's— goes on for the whole day on a Saturday and we had quite good weather, so it was nice.

Unit 18   Keeping fit and healthy

Track 42

Holly	And what about … um … the size of the gym and the size of the pool? Are they quite— quite big?
Receptionist	Um, we have two rooms in the gym. We have one room for the <u>exercises</u> [*Uh-huh.*] and the other side is for the <u>weightlifting</u>
Holly	Right.
Receptionist	And they have bike section for the <u>aero-biking</u>, as well. [*Okay.*] And also they have <u>mirrors</u>.
Holly	Okay, my favourite— Um, I really like going running. Do they have quite a lot of <u>treadmills</u> there?
Receptionist	Yeah, quite a few.
Holly	All right, that's really good. And what about the pool? What's …?
Receptionist	The pool is twenty-five metres.
Holly	Right.
Receptionist	We have … um … lanes, we have three <u>lanes</u>. [*Uh-huh.*] But obviously when we have swimming lessons or in the middle of the day, might be a bit busy because the kids are there. [*Right, okay.*] So after work, about eight o clock [*Okay.*] till we close, is quite [*Okay.*] calm then.
Holly	Cool, and in the lane swims, do you have different speeds?
Receptionist	Yeah.
Holly	So if you wanna go slow, you can go in the slow lane …
Receptionist	Medium and fast, yeah.
Holly	Good, that's useful I think. Alright, well … um …this sounds great, it's a good package. I'd really like to sign up. Can you tell me what information you need from me in order to do that?
Receptionist	Yeah. Um, all we need … um … is obviously just ID, so that's like— something like your passport and … uh … a bill with your address.
Holly	Okay, perfect. That sounds great.
Receptionist	Yeah, and then we can sign you up.
Holly	Great, thank you very much.
Receptionist	Okay then, thank you.

Track 43

Holly	So I mean, I'm never really sure if I should be eating, or what I should be eating before I do exercise or if I should be eating more after I've done exercise. So if you go in an evening after work, I— I'm never quite sure what …
Fitness instructor	Okay, so after work, then we'd say that you've— you've had lunch and dinner then? [Uh-huh.] Um, breakfast, lunch …
Holly	Yeah, and nothing else.
Fitness instructor	… probably not dinner. Okay, so maybe a— a bar or something of … uh … breakfast bar something like that, something— or some nuts, raisins, anything like that [Uh-huh.] to start with.
Holly	Just for energy.
Fitness instructor	Yeah, just for a bit energy. And then after you've finished …uh … your work out, then you'd probably eat something a bit more balanced.
Holly	Okay.
Fitness instructor	Me, personally— I— you— you can eat anything but it's just up to … uh … just how mu— how much and what time you eat it. [Uh-huh.] So I wouldn't tell you that you can't eat this or can't eat that, but obviously watch the amount and the times when you're having it. [Uh-huh.] It's best to just eat <u>in proportion</u>. [Uh-huh.] Try and leave the car at home a bit more [Uh-huh.] and if you— i— you know, if you're— if you're travelling, if it's not too far, obviously you would walk. Forget about the lifts, take the stairs – just things like that. When you're sitting down, make sure you got a good <u>posture</u>, no <u>slumping</u> and things like that, I would try and get over to them, yeah. [Mm.] They— they gonna feel a— feel better within theirself – probably less tired, less pain, and th— they'll naturally wanna do more 'cos they feel like doing more. You know, they b— they're just generally getting more active.

Track 44

Um, I think the— the main drive for me to attend the gym and to keep healthy is, you know, I look around and a lot of men sort of get to fifty years old and they have big pot bellies and they've really let themselves go and, you know, I— I don't wanna be in that position. Um, I don't know, maybe somewhat you could put it down to <u>vanity</u>, I don't know. But … um … you know, at the same point, I don't want to be forty years old when I eventually start a family and not be able to kick the ball around with my son or, you know, go for family walks because I'm overweight or— or unhealthy. Um, plus, I— I think, you know, it just… puts me in a better <u>state of mind</u>. Um, you know, work can be a little— well, everyday living can be stressful. I think i— it's good to sort of get to the gym an— and let out a lot of stresses. Um, you know, I don't think anybody actually enjoys going to the gym. Well, I know I don't really enjoy it. But once you're there, you just kind of go into automatic mode and you go through the motions and, you know, when you leave, you actually do— I do— I feel ten times better. And yeah, it just helps me sort of release stress and gives me energy to just <u>cope</u> with everyday life.

Unit 19   Eating in and eating out

Track 45

And then one night, I went to a Korean barbecue place which I walked past and the smell was so fantastic. I was a little bit nervous of going in, 'cos it was up some stairs and the menu was in Korean and I thought— well, I wasn't quite sure what I was gonna find there. But having walked around looking for somewhere to eat for a bit longer, I thought, 'Actually, that place smelled so good, I'm gonna c— try and find it again and I'm gonna be brave. I'm gonna go in and I'm gonna eat there on my own,' and I did and it was fantastic. I was very lucky, 'cos I'd downloaded a guide to Seoul on my iPod Touch, so I had a little bit about Korean <u>cuisine</u>, because I don't think I would have known what to do with the dish when it came. But fortunately, the— the guidebook that I had on my iPod told me what to do, which is that you take some lettuce, you put the barbecued meat – which has been barbecued in front of you by the waitress in this little <u>pit</u> in the table where they bring the hot <u>coals</u> and they pull the <u>extractor fan</u> down from the— the <u>ceiling</u> – and you— so you put the meat that's been cooked there into the lettuce leaf, you wrap it up, you can choose some *kimchi* which you get with everything in Korea, which is … um … sort of pickled cabbage – which is delicious, actually – and there are other various things you can put in this lettuce leaf and so you can have a different kind of flavour every time. But I had a lot of fun. I was on— there on my own. I was a bit <u>self-conscious</u> about that, but the waitress and I understood each other just enough to … uh …to order and pay and I was very pleased I'd been brave enough to go in.

Track 46

Um, because Simon works for himself, he works from home mostly. So I have to be honest and say my dinner is ready for me most evenings. So … um … it tends to be a mixture. Si— Simon's very … um … regimented so there's a few things he can cook and can cook well, so I try and get him to <u>veer</u> off the— the norm, from time to time. Um, so we'd have things like, you know, your usual pasta dishes, curry dishes, roasts, chicken salads, you know, things like that. Um, and then when I'd go to cook at the weekends, I'd do the more traditional things that you'd get back home, so the bacon and cabbage is a big one, or a stew is a big one, and you know … um … uh … sweet and savoury … uh … salads and things like that. Um, so we— we're sort of very basic cooking at home, because I don't do a lot of it and I don't <u>profess</u> to be the world's greatest chef either.

Um, we tend to go out a lot. There's just the two of us so we like to go out and socialize, so we'll go out with family and we'll go out with friends and— and it's— it's a varied mixture. I like to try new things, so we— for instance, last weekend, we met with our old neighbours that we used to live beside and we went to an Italian restaurant across the road from them which is really, really nice. But at the same time, this weekend we're going out with more friends and we're going to a <u>bistro</u> which is more English food …

Track 47

Yeah in the past I've had a few favourite restaurants… um… Uh, there was a nice little Thai restaurant which was down the road from where I lived back in Sydney and … uh … it was just a nice family— runner— run— just a small place. And, I guess— the— the food was great, but more than anything, I liked the service there. And— and the guy that owned the restaurant was really friendly and, you know, treated us like family, so we— we'd keep going back. And we would recommend it to— to other people – to other friends and …

Unit 20   Sport

Track 48

Uh, touch rugby is … um … a form of rugby which is … uh … far simpler than— than the full rugby union game. It can be used as a training exercise … um … primarily for people who don't— … um … don't really want to get into the <u>full contact</u> side of the game, because rugby is a very physical game. Um, so instead of full <u>tackling</u> and— and putting people on the ground and stepping on them in— in the <u>mud</u> … um … you just touch them with— with both hands and … um … and then the game stops … um … very quickly and— and the ball is recycled – so it's— it's passed back to … um … to your teammates. Um, that will happen five or six times, depending on— on what rules you're playing and then the ball, if there isn't— if there's been no <u>score</u>, then the ball will go over to the other side. So … um … so it's much gentler game … um … it's very, very quick uh … and um … and exciting to play, but it's much less physical. Um, so it's— so it can be played by … um …, by men and women together, it can be played by— … um … by children … um … and it's— it's really good to have a mixed game actually and— and you can get a lot of … um … uh … mixed skill sets playing— playing in the same game … um … without too much <u>damage</u> to— to <u>reputation</u> or to— or to body.

Just— skiing – I'm crazy about skiing. I just wanna do skiing every day. Of— The first time, to be honest, it for me was quite difficult because … um … my parents never skied before. So I didn't have this kind of culture in f— my family to go skiing. And my mum I remember signed me up for the winter holiday in Czech Republic, and I actually took from my gran – sorry, from my godmother – a very long, old-fashioned skis.

And I remember on the climb up, on the top of the slope, and I tried to ski first time and I absolutely loved this and I remember the— the skis, they didn't have um … like a proper stoppers, you know, like a professional one. And so I have to shout at my friends like, you know, 'Be careful!' because the ski was coming down! So I— I almost killed my friends at the same time, but I— and after that when I got back home I said to my mum, 'I really would like to ski,' and my mum managed to actually send me every winter to Czech Republic for one or two weeks' holiday, for proper skiing and with proper instructors, so …

So, if you would like to start skiing, all you need to do and probably the easiest way to do it— it, you just need to go to a proper ski resort and you need to have a proper instructor, because you could learn on your own for ten years and you will be at the same level. And the thing is, with— skiing is very similar to playing golf actually, just because it's very technical. So if you don't have the proper … uh … technique to actually ski or play golf, you wouldn't be able to progress and you will learn skiing or play golf with the mistakes you can repeat over and over again and you never go further, never. So I think proper instructor …

Big sport in Quebec? Well, it's also the big sport in Canada. It's hockey, of course. This— It's a religion. Um, we follow every match re— <u>religiously</u> – every night when we can. Uh, we gather, we go in families, … uh … we— when you have a hockey ticket, like to go to the stadium, we're like— we're like, 'Oh my God, you got a ticket! So lucky!'

It's really easy for us to play hockey. You just need a stick, some— some snow or ice, and a <u>puck</u> and that's it. So yeah, it's really a big part of our history. Uh, I don't know why it's not popular in the rest of the world. I think it's an amazing— it's an— it's more interesting, it's more <u>dynamic</u> than football, … uh … which— way more entertaining, less dramas. When someone falls down, he doesn't cry, he just go back— just go back up and… the match goes on. It don— It— Well, I wouldn't say never stops. It— it stops at time too, but it's like five seconds. Not 'okay everybody, fifteen seconds' and shoot off, and … So, yeah.